6.00
CD25

W9-BLZ-662

REAGANOMICS:

THE NEW FEDERALISM

edited by CARL LOWE

THE REFERENCE SHELF

Volume 55   Number 5

THE H. W. WILSON COMPANY

New York   1984

THE REFERENCE SHELF

The books in this series contain reprints of articles, excerpts from books, and addresses on current issues and social trends in the United States and other countries. There are six separately bound numbers in each volume, all of which are generally published in the same calendar year. One number is a collection of recent speeches; each of the others is devoted to a single subject and gives background information and discussion from various points of view, concluding with a comprehensive bibliography. Books in the series may be purchased individually or on subscription.

Library of Congress Cataloging in Publication Data

Main entry under title:

Reaganomics : the new federalism.

(The Reference shelf ; v. 55, no. 5)
Bibliography: p.
1. United States—Economic policy—1981-   —Addresses, essays, lectures.   2. United States—Social policy—1980-   —Addresses, essays, lectures.   I. Lowe, Carl.
II. Series.
HC106.8.R424   1984   338.973   83-26108
ISBN 0-8242-0688-6

Printed in the United States of America

CONTENTS

PREFACE

"In the first year of his Presidency, Reagan made a strong beginning toward fulfilling [his] mandate. He started getting government off the backs of Americans by reducing a part of the federal budget. He also laid the groundwork for increased investment through tax reductions that put more money in the hands of those who can save and invest it."

These words are from a recent speech by Robert Cizik, President and Chief Executive of Cooper Industries, explaining what he considers to be the heart of Reagan's New Federalism, also known as "Reaganomics."

Ronald Reagan was elected President in 1980 on a platform that emphasized the goal of "getting government off the backs of Americans." It was a platform that the conservative wing of the Republican party embraced wholeheartedly. For many years, conservatives had argued that the Federal government was a monster, growing and out of control, wasting taxpayers' money by creating large bureaucracies that accomplished little beyond their own perpetuation. In addition, conservatives believed that the Federal government had acquired powers that traditionally belonged to the states.

Taxes, in the conservative view, were too high, discouraging business development and investor initiative. Industries were overregulated, increasing the cost of doing business and in turn driving up the price of goods. Federal poverty programs were very costly, and, so the argument ran, were useless for getting the poor back on their economic feet.

A key element in the conservative argument, one particularly endorsed by Reagan, was the concept of supply-side economics. Supply-side economic theory, also known as incentive economics, argues that a combination of tax cuts and deregulation gives business leaders the necessary capital and stimulus for industrial expansion, which in turn results in economic prosperity. The theory goes on to claim that in this general climate of prosperity the Federal government will take in increased tax revenues despite lower tax rates, because the profits being taxed will have grown so large.

5

In general, liberal politicians and those who lean to the political left disagree with these notions. The economic theory they generally look to is based on the ideas of John Maynard Keynes and is known as Keynesian or demand-side economics. While supply-side economics focuses on helping producers create supplies of goods, Keynesians look to manipulation of demand. For instance, the Keynesian answer to the problem of inflation consists, in part, of raising tax rates—anathema to the supply-side advocates—and reducing government expenditures, a combination that is supposed to reduce demand for goods and thus shrink price levels.

The arguments over Reaganomics and the New Federalism do not stop at the boundaries of economic theory. They also extend to the social effects these policies create among the poor and disadvantaged and to whether the highly touted deregulation efforts have hurt the health and safety of Americans and the environment.

Reagan's critics claim that the administration's policies are a cleverly disguised effort to help the rich make more money at the expense of the rest of society. While they admit that Reagan's tax reductions give tax breaks to all classes of citizens, they point out that the largest benefits go to people with high incomes and to large corporations. While the rich get tax breaks, critics point out, assistance to the poor is being cut.

The Reagan counter-argument to this is that the program cuts are mainly intended to eliminate waste and fraud and that a "safety net" of social programs is preserved that safeguards the truly needy from total destitution. It is further claimed that many people on welfare do not need public assistance and should be economically self-sufficient. Allowing them to remain on welfare, President Reagan contends, merely encourages their dependence on public funds and does nothing to cure the causes of poverty.

However, critics of these cuts in Federal social programs object that the main victims of Reaganomics are often children of the poor, who are deprived of adequate nutrition and other necessities when Washington cuts assistance.

Deregulation has also been the focus of heated political debate. Outspoken proponents of deregulation, such as former Secretary of the Interior James Watt, have angered environmentalists and consumer activists, who see much of the current deregulation as an excuse for giving big business a free hand in industrial production at the expense of consumers and of employee safety.

The Reagan administration, on the other hand, feeling that those who wish to protect the environment have had their way too long, wants to make it easier for companies to lease Federal land for oil drilling and mining. The administration claims that adequate environmental safeguards can be maintained when new land is opened up for development.

Section I of this book examines the theoretical underpinning of Reaganomics and the New Federalism. It also looks at the history of its implementation during President Reagan's first two years in office, focusing on how Reagan's economic theories adapted to the political realities.

Section II discusses the ways in which Reagan has come into conflict with Federal agencies in his efforts to trim Federal regulations and the Federal payroll. Section III describes the effects the new policies have had on different socio-economic groups. There is radical disagreement about who has benefited and who has suffered. The articles in Section IV deal with the future of Reaganomics. Some political observers feel that the President himself, far from "staying the course," has begun to abandon his own policies.

The compiler wishes to thank the authors and publishers who have courteously allowed permission for the reprinting of their materials.

Carl Lowe

September 1983

I. REAGANOMICS: THEORY AND IMPLEMENTATION

EDITOR'S INTRODUCTION

A basic tenet of Reaganomics is the necessity for shrinking Federal spending and Federal bureacracy. Advocates of these policies often speak of the futility of "throwing money" at social problems. That's how they characterize policies like those of the late President Lyndon Johnson in pursuit of the "Great Society." According to their theories, the money Johnson spent on anti-poverty programs would have been better left in the hands of the public and never claimed by the Federal government as taxes. That way, these funds would have helped further commerce and industrial development as people and businesses spent it in the private sector.

After President Reagan was elected, he lost no time putting his economic and political ideas into action. One of his most important programs, a three-year tax cut, was passed by the Senate and the House of Representatives almost completely intact (or so it seemed). Many of his budget proposals, which reduced funding for a large group of Federal programs, also seemed to survive the legislative process virtually unscathed.

Melville J. Ulmer, a professor of economics at the University of Maryland, outlines the fundamental differences between Reagan's supply-side economics and Keynesian theory. Writing in *Commentary,* Professor Ulmer shows why neither theory can solve all of our economic ills.

Next, Robert Cizik, president and chief executive officer of Cooper Industries, expresses a great deal of optimism in a speech given to the Southern Hardware Convention. Cizik believes that sticking to Reaganomics and supply-side ideals will cure many of our present problems. According to Cizik, our main need is to reduce the role of government.

Richard P. Nathan, professor of public and international affairs at Princeton, shows how Reaganomics and the New Federalism were born in movements like California's Proposition 13. In an article from *Society,* Professor Nathan calls this movement a retrenchment that has progressed upward through the local, state, and national levels of government.

An article from *Time* magazine describes Reagan's efforts to turn over many Federal programs to the states. The article examines the issue of whether or not this policy actually transfers power to the states to carry out the programs or is merely "fobbing them off in the expectation that many of them would soon die."

WHAT ECONOMISTS KNOW[1]

Vigorous disputes are common among experts in the natural sciences but normally erupt at the unexplored frontiers, when critical facts or experiments are lacking. Not so in economics. Disagreements persist today over fundamental relationships, basic "laws," and hoary doctrines, some of which have been around for a century or more. Furthermore, they survive intransigently, in the face of about as much empirical and theoretical knowledge as can most likely be assembled now or in the foreseeable future. There is no denying that passions are involved, often in the most respected circles. At stake are political commitments as well as academic reputations, emotions as well as fame, against which the reputed dispassionate harmony of scholarly academe is as ineffectual as a parasol in a hurricane. It is as though the economics profession were torn asunder by profound divisions of faith, impervious to the appeals of reason.

Consider, for example, Nobel laureates Milton Friedman and Friedrich Hayek on the one side, and Nobel laureates Paul Samuelson and James Tobin on the other. Despite the impeccable credentials of each, and despite the fervor each publicly exhibits in his views, the two sides agree on practically nothing. Staunchly, they have remained in these opposing positions for at least two decades. Nor does either group suggest that it awaits only the ap-

[1]Magazine article by Melville J. Ulmer, professor of economics at at the University of Maryland. *Commentary.* p 53–57. Jl. '82. Reprinted from *Commentary* July 1982 by permission; all rights reserved.

pearance of some new and critical data for verification. They insist they know the answers now. Clearly one side or the other must be wrong, or both.

Nor is the reason for such stubborn wrangling simply the impenetrability of the subject matter, the scarcity of dependable knowledge, or the impossibility (in the social sciences generally) of settling disputes with controlled experiments. Economics has been called "the queen of the social sciences" just because most of its variables are quantifiable. With millions of government clerks grinding out mountains of statistics daily, there is no dearth of factual information. The rules of logic are as readily accessible to economists as to anyone else. Persuasive evidence would appear to be serviceably at hand to confirm or deny many economic propositions. Even experiments of a kind are possible which, while not strictly controlled, can be repeated in varying situations. What remains in opposition are articles of faith, precious to particular "schools" of thought, in which political biases as well as personal advantages are heavily invested.

Examples abound of disputes that range beyond reason, but most of these center around the fundamental clash in social philosophy that splits the four economists named above. It is the critical contest for economic policy today, engaging conservative classicists on the Right and liberals of various hues on the Left. Most prominent among the latter are neo-Keynesians, or economic "demand-siders," who more or less dominated the nation's social strategy from 1948 until 1980. "Other things being equal"—as they are wont to say—they favor governmental decision-making over the market. They long for a progressive "leveling" in the distribution of income. Their eager opponents are the "supply-siders" who moved to center stage with the Reagan administration. The more extreme among them favor the market over government almost to the point of old-time laissez-faire. Substantial inequalities in income, allowing incentives for effort and ambition, are in their eyes essential not only for industrial progress but for individual freedom.

Both Right and Left support opposing pet theories for stabilizing the economy, to which they cling despite past experience that most bystanders would consider discouraging. Their efforts to avoid cycles of inflation and depression were given long and loving trials in turn, one in the decades before 1932 and one later, with results that in public estimation ranged from deeply disturbing to disastrous. Naturally, both sides question that evaluation, at least as it bears on their own strategies, on the ground that in one significant detail or another their advice was disregarded. Another possible view is that of George J. W. Goodman (a.k.a. "Adam Smith") who recently wrote: "Having been part of the solution, economics has become part of the problem."

In its broadest terms, supply-side economics goes back to (the original) Adam Smith, and with modification here or there has remained a part of Western tradition ever since. Irving Kristol has summarized its five "bedrock truths" as follows:

(1) The overwhelming majority of men and women are naturally and incorrigibly interested in improving their material conditions; (2) efforts to repress this natural desire lead only to coercive and impoverished politics; (3) when this natural desire is given sufficient latitude so that commercial transactions are not discouraged, economic growth does take place; (4) as a result of such growth, everyone does eventually indeed improve his condition, however unequally in extent or time; (5) such economic growth results in a huge expansion of the property-owning middle class—a necessary (though not sufficient) condition for a liberal society in which individual rights are respected.

Probably the vast majority of Americans, with the principal exception of the intellectual Left, would accept these tenets as consistent with personal experience and the lessons of history. There is much less agreement about their specific implications for public policy. How far can and should we go toward providing full leeway for individual self-interest and the unrestricted decisions of the free market? Perhaps the most controversial of all the supposed injunctions is the admonition that we must abide by Say's Law.

This so-called law, named for an early expositor of Smith, states that *supply creates its own demand.* No one would produce, said Jean Baptiste Say two centuries ago, without an intention to consume or invest the proceeds. Therefore, the income generated by production—in wages, salaries, profits, etc.—must always be just enough to purchase the supply. A general glut of output, in that setting, is impossible—a proposition which inevitably provokes the question, what of depressions? The answer is that in the earliest days of modern capitalism, with free-market activities only in the process of spreading, business cycles were unknown, though of course there were problems to spare aside from that. Writing in the closing decade of the 18th century, Say undoubtedly meant the law to apply in the *long run,* as possibly it does. It was the later economists of the 19th and 20th centuries who converted the broad, impressionistic Smithian theory into a tight, purely abstract mathematical model.

Modern versions of the old classical theory exchange the keen though casual observations of its founders for the precise postulations and impeccable deductions of Euclidean geometry. In such models of the economy, time is ruled out, reactions are assumed to be instantaneous, and the actors—buyers and sellers—are presumed to have perfect knowledge in perfectly competitive markets. Hence, in the short run as well as the long run those who wish to do so can "prove" that a free economy will gravitate naturally toward full employment without inflation. Were goods to remain unsold, to the temporary discomfort of producers, either of two correctives would quickly appear. Prices would decline, thus encouraging purchases, or, since consumers were spending less, they would save and invest more. In either case, full employment would be preserved, and the possibility of a cumulative slide, with falling sales leading to lower incomes and investment, would be effectively excluded. Efforts by government to intervene are therefore held to be self-defeating. For example, defensive fiscal or monetary measures would only worsen the impact of an "exogenous shock" (like the 1929 stock market crash) by blocking natural forces of recovery. So says Say's Law, and to this day many learned heads nod in solemn acquiescence, both in academe and in the federal offices of the more pietistic supply-siders.

But there are other supply-siders besides the pietistic ones. Pulling and tugging within the broad official or unofficial entourage of the Reagan administration are three distinguishable groups. Budget balancers like David Stockman, Herbert Stein, and Arthur Burns believe that the principal key to enduring prosperity is to cut government spending down to the level of tax revenue. Monatarists like Milton Friedman and Beryl Sprinkel are convinced that the overriding need is to grasp control of the money supply, limiting its growth to the long-run advance of productivity and population. Tax reducers like Arthur Laffer, Paul Craig Roberts, Norman Ture, and Jack Kemp believe that cutting taxes radically would unleash a flood of work energy, investment, and innovation that would swiftly revitalize the economy, balance the budget, and reduce unemployment and inflation to the status of unpleasant memories. Obviously President Reagan has borrowed something from all three groups, though not to the full satisfaction of any one of them.

What supply-siders in general have in common are (1) their firm rejection of "demand-side" neo-Keynesian economics; (2) their classical emphasis on the central role of individual enterprise and business investment in generating economic progress; and (3) their belief in the approximate validity of Say's Law—although here the more pragmatic budget balancers, like Stein and Burns, take highly qualified or dissenting positions. Toward the first two points, public sentiment has grown preponderantly favorable, though no doubt weakened somewhat by the 1981–82 recession. On the third, both a large part of the public and their elected representatives would manifestly be wary. At any rate there is an obligation to test this plank, as well as the first, against whatever evidence history can afford. Just how strong, in fact, are the natural recuperative powers of a free economy?

When we look back at the record for evidence, the plight of the unfortunate Herbert Hoover in 1929 looms like a pyramid in the Giza desert. He consulted the leading economists of his time, ultra-conservatives all. His public assurance that prosperity was "just around the corner," issued on their authority, was dutifully repeated for the next three years. Obtuseness perhaps, but not callousness, accounts for his failure to do much else but talk in history's greatest economic crisis. For Hoover shared an abiding faith with Joseph Schumpeter, Frank Knight (Milton Friedman's mentor), Jacob Viner, Friedrich Hayek, Irving Fisher, and most other economic luminaries of the day. Specifically, the faith was in Say's Law.

The relevant evidence, however, does not start and stop with the Great Depression. From the 1870's through the 1920's, an era of almost unqualified laissez-faire, three giant depressions (excluding that of the 1930's) plus sixteen smaller but severe contractions shook the nation with the customary spasms of mass unemployment, foreclosures, and bankruptcies.* All the larger business cycles were worldwide; and in two instances—Italy and Germany—they were fatal. In the most abundantly documented study of this experience, Wesley Clair Mitchell, America's foremost authority on business cycles, demonstrated what Karl Marx from an entirely different point of view had only surmised: that a private enterprise economy moves *naturally* in waves. One phase of a business cycle inescapably gives rise to the next in a "self-generating" oscillation. Typically, economic expansions generate a surge of investment that cannot possibly be sustained, while in downturns unsatisfied (and often unpostponable) demands accumulate.

But this is but one of a myriad of synergistically interrelated impulses, unraveled by Mitchell, that mold the cyclical pattern of business. It is mainly the timing and the intensity of the fluctuations that vary. Ominously, he found, the major cycles alternate unpredictably with the smaller ones. Whatever support there is for Say's Law must be located in stubborn hope or in the arcane mathematics of abstract, otherworldly speculative theories.**

For their part, the neo-Keynesians on the Left have been equally disdainful of what most bystanders might consider readily available evidence. They have clung just as tenaciously to what must be termed a professionally exalted myth. The unplanned legacy of the great John Maynard Keynes was what came to be, after World War II, the dominant school led by Samuelson, Tobin, Walter Heller, the late Arthur Okun, and Lawrence Klein. This group proclaimed—and most of its members still do—that the business cycle is dead in theory and *ought* to be dead in fact. Their knowledge of fiscal and monetary policy, they say, would enable

*All according to the National Bureau of Economic Research, the national arbiter in recording business cycles.
**One of the earliest mathematic models of the kind, and certainly the most famous, is that of Leon Walras (1837-1910), hailed by Joseph Schumpeter as the greatest economist of all time. My own choice would be David Ricardo, followed closely by Smith and more distantly by Keynes and Mitchell.

them to maintain a virtually unaltered state of full employment without inflation, *if only* the politicians of this world would heed their advice with sufficient alacrity.

But once again the awkward record of history conflicts with shallow hopes and theoretical speculation. How valid can the neo-Keynesian claim be when its advice was influential as early as the 1950's and then officially dominant during the next twenty years? Remember that even President Nixon, with only semi-jocular innocence, asked, "Aren't we all Keynesians now?" In his brief term of office President Ford displayed similar credentials, though gracelessly unacknowledged by conventional liberals. Under Kennedy, Johnson, and Carter, the neo-Keynesians themselves occupied the official drivers' seats. That long-term experiment should be enough to discredit what Heller and his colleagues, in their halcyon days, proclaimed to be the "New Economics."

In the thirty-two years from 1948 to 1980 there were eight recessions of generally increasing gravity, with unemployment rising to progressively higher peaks. Most disturbing of all was the swiftly mounting inflation which started walking in the 1950's, trotting in the 1960's, and galloping in the next decade. Throughout the entire period since World War II the price level rose in every year except two: 1949 and 1954. From 1950 to 1980, consumer prices rose by 350 percent. In the fateful last two years of that period the average annual inflation rate was 13 percent—enough to double the cost of living in less than six years—while unemployment hovered between 6 and 8 percent of the labor force. There was no way, without blatantly courting disaster, that the conventional Keynesian measures could be used to combat either inflation or unemployment, and certainly not both at the same time. One positive credit that President Reagan deserves is that he did not try that route.

The fatal error of the neo-Keynesians was the mirror image of that of the supply-siders. Their hang-up was and is Keynes's Law: that *demand* creates its own *supply*. It was a dictum that the master had devised for the Great Depression, hardly a typical situation. The stunning extravagance of the neo-Keynesians was to generalize. Their resulting policy prescription, enshrined in all but some of the more recent textbooks, is worth repeating here.

When unemployment threatens to be excessive, any one or all of the following three actions are indicated: increase government expenditures, reduce taxes, and/or expand the money supply to lower the rate of interest. These measures, of course, are supposed to raise demand and lift employment. When inflation appears, the prescription calls for the opposite tack: reduce government expenditures, elevate tax rates, and/or contract the money supply to raise the rate of interest. These tactics, they thought, should reduce demand and lower the price level.

In practice, the prescription was followed with reasonable precision for thirty years. Even the conservative and—so it was thought—economically naive President Eisenhower jiggled defense expenditures with an eye to their impact on demand and the general level of business activity. From then on, the neo-Keynesian formula in full was gospel. But unfortunately for the nation, demand stubbornly refused to create its own supply. More reliably, it raised the price level. The result was the well-known roller-coaster pattern in which ever-eager "stabilizers" fought inflation by provoking unemployment, then fought unemployment by provoking inflation, only to find that from one cycle to the next both were getting worse.

We must note for the sake of completeness that after a time neo-Keynesians conceded that something else was needed—something other than their fiscal and monetary formula. Their answer was an "incomes policy," by which they have meant some form of "voluntary" wage and price controls, along with—a point emphasized by some more than others—a judicious use of income taxes and the welfare system to siphon more income from the richer to the poorer. But as any wide-awake observer knows, all these devices were put into practice, especially in the Kennedy, Johnson, and Carter administrations, and in one respect Nixon went a step further, with *mandatory* wage-price controls. However, no discernible improvement in result was evident. The voluntary systems of direct control reliably crumbled just when they were needed, as soon as demand pressure mounted in a period of expansion. Nixon's experiment confirmed a long-established verity: that once mandatory controls are dismantled, as sooner or later they must be, the result is a price explosion worse than the one temporarily suppressed.

In a profession in which fixations seem the rule rather than the exception, it should come as no surprise that such failures have served to invigorate rather than still the liberal call for more government intervention. Nor could it have been unexpected that, interspersed with hurried rebuttals to the Republican response, there would be cries of moral "outrage," more unrestrained as one moves leftward in the neo-Keynesian political spectrum toward radicals and the penumbra of Marx. Robert Lekachman, for example, finds that President Reagan's primary political objective is to "enrich the already obscenely rich," a passage that might have been borrowed from a dog-eared copy of *Left-Wing Orations for all Occasions*. In his latest book, *Greed Is Not Enough*, Lekachman summarizes his own, "progressive" program as a "mandatory incomes policy, political direction of investment, redistributive taxation, and . . . democratic planning."

In this work as well as in those of others on Lekachman's side, tempers flare most notably at the thought of income inequalities. Even so experienced a practitioner as Lester Thurow of MIT can excitably use statistics on this point with the skill of a free-spirited high-school debater. "Welfare," he explained to an audience in 1980, "constitutes only 1.2 percent of the GNP." But according to the Social Security administration, the true figure is 20 percent of the GNP, and also 60 percent of the combined federal, state, and local budget, including in "welfare" Aid to Families with Dependent Children, Medicaid, food stamps, training programs, unemployment insurance, housing assistance, public-service employment, child nutrition, food distributions, and scores of related outlays. Of all these programs and the others not listed, Thurow must have stopped counting when he came to the first. To the question, "How much equality do I want?" Lekachman (in concert with Thurow, Tobin, Herbert J. Gans, Gar Alperovitz, and other associates) answers: "More!" With greater precision, their late colleague Arthur Okun set an "ethical" goal of *full* "equality in the distribution of incomes," a situation which, if applied to the world (and without the mischief of disincentives and the imprisonment of individual proclivities), would establish a standard income for all humanity at considerably less than one-half the present U.S. official poverty level.

As practical matters for public consideration, the questions raised by those Left of Center could hardly have been less relevant to the problems confronting Ronald Reagan when he took office in January 1981. His economic inheritance was the cumulative burden of all the policy blunders of the preceding twenty years. Its symptoms were stagnant economic growth and the most unfavorable combination of inflation (at a 13 percent annual rate) and unemployment (at more than 7 percent) in modern history. Yet, for him, the legacy was a double-edged bonanza. Without the mess, he never would have been elected. With it, common sense alone dictated the immediate courses of action, however difficult in execution. The bloated deficit had to be reduced, both because of its inflationary impact and the often flabby programs and political irresponsibilities it sheltered. Marginal tax rates on the middle class, inexorably lifted by "bracket creep," had to be moderated to inspire work effort, saving, and investment. Productivity had staggered and then dropped in the preceding decade. For comparable reasons the growing burden of taxes and costly regulations on business had to be eased. The inflationary expansion of the money supply had to be slowed.

True enough, finding the appropriate combination of these measures proved to be difficult, not to mention winning and retaining congressional cooperation. Tight money discouraged investment while tax reductions widened the deficit. The predictable recession raised unemployment as it always does. Further budgetary economies, which might have relieved the pressure in markets for credit, met cagey Democratic opposition after an initial year of détente. Still, the immediate, pressing objective of checking inflation made unexpectedly impressive progress and, by the late spring of 1982, the slide in output and employment had perceptibly slowed.

If the President's ardent hopes are realized and a business recovery without inflation ensues, it may well be safe to say, with a collective sigh, three cheers for the year ahead—since expansions seldom last less than a year. But it would probably be safer to add to common sense, "Thank you, I'll call again when I need you." For there is a remaining question that could haunt us all, that calls distinctly for uncommon sense: what next?

What will follow if, as the Reagan administration hopes and intends, a reasonable framework for economic progress is put in place, including refreshed incentives, a prudently managed budget, and an effective rein on the money supply? Granted that, together, they would inspire productivity and set a friendly stage for long-term investment. Can they also curb the destructive spates of instability that have plagued Western society since the industrial revolution? History seems to say that the unpredictable bouncing ball of cyclical fluctuations does not come to rest so easily.

Business cycles, in short, have been a reality in the past and are part of the future prospect of any private-enterprise economy. Wishing, and a faith in Say's Law, will not make them go away. Neither, however, will a return to the rituals of neo-Keynesian economics. The utopian dream of wiping them out, precious to radical "planners," is no more feasible than curing a headache with decapitation. A totalitarian state could do it, but only with its own style of social surgery. The alternative, in a free-economy, is to learn to ride the waves of business activity without the precarious pitches and rolls of unemployment and inflation. That requires institutional strength and resiliency; whether the Reagan administration can establish these qualities over the longer term remains to be seen.

THE CHALLENGE OF LESS GOVERNMENT[2]

I would like to begin my talk today with a quotation. As I read these words I would like you to think about who said them and about what country.

I sit on a man's back choking him and making him carry me, and yet assure myself and others that I am very sorry for him and wish to ease his lot by all possible means—except by getting off his back.

[2] Address by Robert Cizik, president and chief executive officer of Cooper Industries, to the Southern Hardware Convention, Houston, Texas, April 19, 1982. *Vital Speeches of the Day.* 48:523–525. Je. 15, '82. Reprinted by permission.

If you guessed Ronald Reagan and the United States, you were wrong. Those words were used by Leo Tolstoi to describe Russian society prior to the Bolshevik Revolution.

Does it bother you that we can so easily confuse Leo Tolstoi's criticism of tzarist Russia with Ronald Reagan's criticism of democratic America? I know it bothers me. How did we get this way? More important, what are we willing to do about it? Are we prepared to cast the burden of big government off our backs and meet the challenge that implies?

Most observers agree that the United States government began its inexorable growth in 1932 with the election of Franklin Delano Roosevelt as President. As he was inaugurated, depression, unemployment, and despair were crushing the nation. America desperately needed change, and Roosevelt set out to provide that change. With enormous energy, the new administration labored to create a myriad of programs, plans and projects . . . the Social Security Administration, the National Recovery Administration, the Public Works Administration, and the Civilian Conservation Corps were just a few. . . . The New Deal was born.

Fifty years later, economists are still debating whether the New Deal worked. True, the depression ended. But many students of that period insist that the upturn resulted largely from rearmament in Europe and the United States—and from World War II—not from Roosevelt's spending programs.

But whether the programs worked or not, the New Deal's impact on American history was revolutionary—revolutionary because a belief was born. Americans saw that prosperity returned when government grew: Americans *believed* that prosperity returned *because* government grew. And that perception became the foundation for fifty years of increasing federal spending.

Shakespeare, in *All's Well That Ends Well,* said, "Great floods have flown from simple sources." The flood that flowed from the New Deal brought Washington's share of our gross national product from 3 percent in 1929 to 20 percent today.

If America's romance with more government began with the New Deal, that romance blossomed during the Second World War. World War II was a popular war. Our cause was just; our people were united against a common enemy; and our armies emerged victorious . . . victorious and unravaged . . . unravaged and strong . . . strong and in sole possession of nuclear weapons . . . ready to defend freedom in the Cold War era. America's faith and confidence in its government soared.

That confidence continued to rise for two more decades—as we passed from Roosevelt's New Deal to Truman's Fair Deal to Kennedy's New Frontier and Johnson's Great Society. I omit Eisenhower, not because he was innocent of contributing to our growing government, but because his administration was less creative in coming up with a catchy slogan to ennoble its activities. Those activities, deals, frontiers, and societies spanned the decades from 1945 to 1965—decades that were blessed with extraordinary growth and prosperity.

As in Roosevelt's time, that prosperity coincided with increasing government involvement. We wonder, however, whether that economic expansion was dependent on government's actions. We wonder whether that growth *didn't* result from Americans' spending the savings they had been forced to accumulate during the war . . . spending those savings on goods they had wanted to purchase since the beginning of the depression.

Whatever their true cause, those two decades of prosperity transformed America's romance with government into absolute, unquestioning devotion. By the mid-sixties, we became convinced that the powers of Washington were boundless—that the economists could fine-tune the economy—that almost any social ill could be cured by launching another federal program—and that we could pursue those programs at the same time that we fought a land war in Asia . . . guns and butter . . . the war in Vietnam and the war on poverty.

Lyndon Johnson expressed a firmly held American belief when he said, "We have the opportunity to move not only toward the rich society and the powerful society but upward to the Great Society."

Sadly, that belief was wrong, and the price of the mistake was great. The mid-sixties mark both the pinnacle of our unquestioning support for the actions of government, and the beginning of our fall into a period of deep disillusionment. In the nightmare of that fall, we suffered endless frustrations over Vietnam and serious disappointments from the failures of the Great Society program. We endured Watergate and Abscam and a series of economic cycles that appeared to be of ever increasing severity. Today, we face an economy that's wallowing in a productivity malaise at the same time that it's struggling with foreign competition and fighting the lethargy of recession. Some people would substitute the word depression for recession. And, for at least certain industries—those sensitive to our soaring interest rates—few would argue the point.

It was Alphonse Karr, the French journalist and novelist, who said: "The more things change, the more they remain the same." Roosevelt first ventured on the path of more government because he was searching for ways to ease the suffering of the Great Depression. Now, after fifty years of following that path, things have changed, but in many ways they remain the same. Again the nation is suffering—suffering from unemployment and despair. And again we are searching. But this time the search is not for federal programs which promise to ease our pain. This time the search is for less government.

The search started in the mid-sixties—it started in the summer of 1964 . . . in San Francisco . . . with the nomination of Barry Goldwater as a candidate for President. Even though Goldwater was soundly trounced in the election, doubts about the role of government had been planted. And those doubts grew.

Jimmy Carter was the first President to be elected by our growing discomfort with big government. His claim to the White House rested on his lack of prior association with the federal government. Carter's supporters believed that an outsider could restrain Washington's appetite for power. Carter disappointed his constituents and they turned away—away from Carter to Reagan. They turned to Reagan because he promised, in no uncertain terms, to reduce the role of the federal government. Americans believed that promise. And they translated their disillusionment with government into a landslide victory—a mandate for change.

In the first year of his Presidency, Reagan made a strong beginning toward fulfilling that mandate. He started getting government off the backs of Americans by reducing a part of the federal budget. He also laid the groundwork for increased investment through tax reductions that put more money in the hands of those who can save and invest it.

But despite Reagan's strong start, our goal of less government is still only a distant hope. Federal spending continues to grow at a vigorous pace—and the gap between outlays and revenues appears wider with each projection. Tax reductions remain under debate—and volumes of regulations are still stifling our industry. In his first year in office, Reagan entered the fray. But the important battles have yet to be fought.

Those battles require a much larger army than just Reagan and his administration. If we are to win, the fight must be joined by all of us. And that fight will not be easy.

In *Alice in Wonderland,* the March Hare invites Alice to take some more tea. She replies that she's had none so she can't take more. To this the Mad Hatter says: "You mean you can't take *less.* It's very easy to take *more.* . . . "

Our situation seems to be very much like Alice's. Whereas it's easy to take more, it's hard to take less. Whereas more government comes almost automatically, less government is a difficult goal. Less government is a challenge.

To meet that challenge, we must approach our task with a clear vision. Today our vision is clouded by certain myths that soften the hard edges of reality but are, in fact, false. One of these myths might be summed up in the phrase, "It will all be over soon." The *Atlantic Monthly*'s infamous article described a device that David Stockman used last year. That device was labeled the "Magic Asterisk." And Stockman used it to dismiss all future concerns about budget deficits. The article said:

"The Magic Asterisk" would blithely denote all future deficit problems that were to be taken care of with additional budget reductions, to be announced by the President at a later date. Thus, everyone could finesse the hard questions, for now.

We are still finessing those hard questions. Like Scarlett O'Hara, we're dismissing our difficulties with the phrase, "I'll think of it tomorrow." We're deluding ourselves into the belief that the struggle to reverse fifty years of government growth will require only a few major battles—certainly not a lengthy siege. In fact, the job of re-establishing our fiscal integrity, of rethinking our national priorities, and of creating the legislation to accurately reflect those priorities will probably require a steady effort throughout the decade of the 80s. Failure to recognize that fact may rob us of the stamina necessary to stay the course. And, before our task is finished, we could find ourselves in the situation described by Cornelius Vanderbilt's great-grandson Alfred when he said:

It is not the knowledge of ways and means we lack: it is the will to put them into effect.

In the course of our long-term effort to reduce government spending, we will, at some point, be forced to abandon our second myth. That myth can be phrased, "Budget cuts should affect only evil people." The definition of evil, like beauty, seems to be "altogether in the eye of the beholder." Conservatives point to welfare cheaters. Liberals accuse the wasteful Pentagon. Both groups attack the burgeoning bureaucracy. But the fact is that there simply aren't enough cuts available from these groups to solve our problems. To establish a sound fiscal footing, we will have to trim programs that benefit people we hold in high regard—people like retirees from the military service and Social Security recipients— our parents, neighbors, perhaps even ourselves.

So far, Reagan's budget cutting has been confined to a small part of the total pie. Entitlements, which make up half of the budget, remain virtually untouched. Defense, which accounts for another fourth, is not being reduced. In fact, it's being increased. After eliminating entitlements and defense, we're left with only a fourth of the budget. Of that 25 percent, 10 percent is interest expense—a cost that really is uncontrollable. And that gets us to the 15 percent that has been subject to attack so far. It's true that great strides have been made in reducing this 15 percent. But as long as we maintain this myopic vision—as long as we look only at 15 percent of the whole—we will never control the spiraling costs of federal spending. The keys to that control are the programs that receive half of the budget's funds. The keys to that control are entitlements.,

I find it interesting that discussions about reducing entitlements always seem to involve anatomical metaphors. Cuts that affect those for whom we have little sympathy invariably do away with "fat." Cuts that affect the groups we favor always slice dangerously into "muscle," possibly even "bone." And any restraint on entitlements benefitting our families, our friends, or ourselves is usually characterized as "butchering" the entire program, "ripping out its heart," or "tearing it limb from limb." But regardless of the words we use, can we really afford all of the laudable but wildly expensive goals that we've embodied in our entitlement programs?

Can we afford a 100 percent indexing scheme for government employees' pensions—a scheme that, after several years, often provides the retired employee with more money than his colleagues still in service? At one point, after retiring, Speaker of the House McCormack received an annual pension of almost $92,-000. His active successor was earning $79,000. Some generals and admirals, who have been out of the military for ten years, now make $64,000. Those currently on duty are getting $54,000.

Civil service and military pensions are only part of the entitlement problem. Another part is Social Security. In 1945, Social Security costs consumed only a little more than a day of America's pay for the year. Since then, that figure has increased by a multiple of 25. This year, we'll work more than six weeks just to cover Social Security benefits and administrative expenses. If allowed to proceed unchecked, the claim on our earnings will double again by the year 2025. At that time, the working American will have to devote 12 weeks—almost three months—of his pay exclusively to the expenses of our Social Security system.

In 1945, there were 50 wage earners to support each member of the Social Security roll. Now, each recipient is supported by about three workers. In 2025, there may be less than two taxpayers for each beneficiary.

What right do we have to burden future generations with that sort of obligation? Can we, within reason, expect those generations to accept that burden? Clearly, responsible adjustments are in order—adjustments, not only to the mechanics of our Social Security System, but most important, adjustments to our expectations about the amount of entitlements we believe we're entitled to receive.

While making these needed adjustments is important, the total challenge of less government is much broader. It consists of redefining the role of our federal government and enacting the legislation to support that definition. In undertaking this challenge, we would do well to be guided by the words of Abraham Lincoln:

The legitimate object of government is to do for a community of people whatever they need to have done, but cannot do at all, or cannot so well do for themselves in their separate and individual capacities. In all that the people can individually do as well for themselves, government ought not to interfere.

Most of what I've been saying today is summed up in that last sentence, "In all that the people can individually do as well for themselves, government ought not to interfere." Those words speak volumes about the role of government in our society. But they also say a great deal about the role of the individual. They say that the people must be *willing* to do individually all that people *can* do individually.

If we are to succeed in reducing the role of government, we must be willing to undertake some difficult tasks—the difficult task of providing for the needs of our community—the difficult task of shouldering the responsibilities for our families—the difficult task of assuming the burdens of our own lives.

RETRENCHMENT COMES TO WASHINGTON[3]

The retrenchment that has occurred in the domestic policies of the U.S. national government should not have surprised us. It had been on the way for a long time. It began at the local level in the mid-seventies, largely as a response to the New York fiscal crisis. Census data show that city governments began to cut spending and reduce employment in that period.

[3] Magazine article by Richard P. Nathan, professor of public and international affairs, Princeton University. Published by permission of Transaction, Inc. from *Society*, Vol. 19, #5. Copyright © 1982 by Transaction, Inc.

Nineteen seventy-eight was actually the turning point. The enactment of Proposition 13 in California in that year was the most important event in signaling the turn to the right that has occurred in domestic affairs in the United States. Although other states had limits on taxes and spending before California did (New Jersey, for example), Proposition 13 erupted like Mount St. Helens, spreading fiscal restraint across the nation. The national government was soon affected. Jimmy Carter tried, with some success, to cut the domestic spending of the government in the budgets of his last two years in office. It is instructive to look at his record.

In 1977, soon after taking office, Carter won quick enactment of a package of stimulus measures to aid the economy in the form of about $13.5 billion in additional spending over three years for three purposes—public service jobs, emergency revenue sharing, and special public works projects. People tend to forget this. What they remember—in that wonderful summary way the human memory works—is that Carter was weak in the field of domestic affairs. They forget the successes.

In 1978, Carter caused a great stir in Washington with what later was to become one of his failures, his national urban policy. Announced with great fanfare, this program would have, in effect, made the 1977 stimulus spending permanent. Carter proposed $4 to $5 billion a year in new urban spending "targeted" to needy communities. The best way to summarize Carter's record in domestic affairs is to say that he had a truly big and bold urban program (the 1977 stimulus package) that lasted just about until the time he announced his national urban program. Then it all fizzled. Why did it fall apart? The answer can be found in the steady eastward movement of retrenchment in our national politics. Carter read the political tea leaves in 1979; he began to lose enthusiasm for, and to move away from, his own urban program. There were some efforts that continued, but Carter's big spending aspirations dimmed after Proposition 13.

Thus, change was already in the air at the time of the 1980 election. Ronald Reagan, aided by the brilliant performance of David Stockman and the opportunity afforded him by the 1974 budget act, turned in a virtuoso performance his first year in office. In much the same way that Carter in 1977 had used the momentum of his election to get new spending, Reagan used the momentum of his election to cut spending. Of the two events, the latter—Reagan's 1981 budget cuts—is by far the more important.

The lower part of the table shows that, in 1972 constant dollars, Carter cut two major areas in the wake of Proposition 13. The pattern for Reagan is similar but more pronounced. In Reagan's first year—fiscal 1982—defense spending was projected to rise by 7.8 percent in real terms. Grants to states and localities for other than welfare purposes were projected to fall much more sharply than in the period from 1978 to 1981. The important new element was a turnabout on welfare grants paid to the states— primarily Aid for Dependent Children (AFDC) and Medicaid. They rose by 5.6 percent per year in constant dollars from 1978 to 1981, and were projected to *fall* by 3.4 percent in these terms in fiscal year 1982. This analysis was done by John W. Ellwood, with a team of students and staff at the Woodrow Wilson School, as the baseline for a study, more fully described later, of the effects of the 1982 domestic budget cuts and related policy changes.

Budget Reconciliation

The Omnibus Budget Reconciliation Act passed in 1981 is the single most important piece of social legislation enacted in the United States since the Social Security Act of 1935. This legislation did not just cut spending; it fundamentally changed social programs. It was not just a spending bill (or, rather, an antispending bill); it contained major changes in a wide range of authorizing laws that affect the essential role of the national government in the social area. Understanding its impact requires turning to a more technical subject, the development of reconciliation in the U.S. budget process.

Reconciliation is the new budget process of the American government. When this process was written into law as section 310 of the 1974 budget act, it was not then clear how it would work. Congress invented the reconciliation process by doing it.

The budget act provides for two budget resolutions each year, one in the spring and one in the fall. The first is supposed to set

GROWTH RATES OF FEDERAL OUTLAYS
DURING THE CARTER YEARS

Type of spending	FY1971– FY1978	FY1978– FY1981	FY1981– FY1982 (estimate)
Annual Percentage Growth in Current Dollars			
National Defense	4.9	15.0	17.4
Payments to individuals	14.9	15.4	11.0
Direct payments	(15.2)	(15.4)	(12.1)
Grant payments	(13.5)	(15.5)	(3.9)
Other state and local grants	17.5	1.9	–9.3
Net interest	13.4	24.8	20.8
All other operations	12.6	5.7	–6.5
Total outlays	11.5	13.6	10.4
Annual Percentage Growth in 1972 Constant Dollars			
National defense	–2.5	4.1	7.8
Payments to individuals	7.9	5.7	3.1
Direct payments	(8.2)	(5.7)	(4.0)
Grant payments	(6.7)	(5.6)	(–3.4)
Other state and local grants	9.3	–6.1	–16.6
Net interest	6.3	14.6	11.5
All other operations	4.1	–3.2	–11.2
Total outlays	4.1	4.0	2.3

Source: Average annual percentage growth rates calculated from outlay data contained in Office of Management and Budget, *Federal Government Finances: 1983 Budget Data.* Growth rate from fiscal year 1981 to fiscal year 1982 is based on the February 1982 OMB estimate of fiscal year 1982 outlays.

nonbinding "targets"; and the second, "ceilings" for spending. Section 310 provides that the second resolution can include "directions" to other committees "to determine and recommend changes to accomplish a change of *such total amount.*" The words *such total amount* refer to the amount that has to be cut to reduce spending to the levels in the second budget resolution. The law further stipulates that, if these directions (now called "instructions") involve more than one committee in either House, then the budget committee of that House "upon receiving all such recommendations, shall report to its House a reconciliation bill or reconciliation resolution, or both, carrying out all such recommendations without substantive revision." Note the three not-so-little words, *without substantive revision.* The budget committee was not supposed to meddle in substance—at least, that was the idea.

Section 310, that seemingly innocuous provision to pull together conforming changes, has become the new budget process of the U.S. government. The process will probably continue to operate this way for a long time. As long as we have to cut, which the 1981 tax reductions and large defense commitments seem to assure us will be required for quite a while, then we need some way to apportion the pain of that surgery. Committees of Congress can spend without coordination, but cutting spending is different; it requires a plan and an agreement or it will not happen.

For the first five years that the congressional budget act was on the books, the reconciliation provision was not used. It was first used in 1980 to allocate about $8 billion in cuts. Then, in 1981, it was taken advantage of with true bravado by the Reagan administration as the vehicle for retrenchment. David Stockman and the Office of Management and Budget staff wrote the Gramm-Latta substitute reconciliation bill and sent it up to the House a few hours before it was voted upon. The president got on the phone from California and lobbied for votes. He won. Now it is a new ballgame.

It is a new ballgame for one primary reason. The major problem for domestic programs, as many see it, is the built-in growth of entitlement programs—like social security, Medicaid, Medicare, AFDC, and food stamps. Not all entitlement programs work the same way, but as a rule they have some kind of permanent au-

thorization, which may or may not require an annual appropria-
tion. Cutting these programs requires the ability to get at the
authorization laws that set forth the rules for entitlement payments. That is precisely what the Gramm-Latta reconciliation bill
did in 1981. It did this—and this is very important—not on the
second budget resolution, but on the first.

We will go though reconciliation each year, and each year will
be different. There is no telling how it will work next year (FY
1984), but if it does not work, the current publicly unacceptable
triple digit federal deficit could double. Since the public appears
to have zero tolerance for the current level of the federal deficit,
there is great pressure on Congress to keep doing reconciliation.

Thus Reagan's 1981 reconciliation victory was a historic piece
of social legislation. Its biggest effect was on the poor—
particularly the working poor who had previously been aided (as
some still are) under various entitlement programs. This group
of poor people, working-aged and able-bodied, is the most controversial welfare group. Many in this group no longer receive
AFDC, food stamps, Medicaid, housing, and other benefits to
supplement their low earnings. The Reagan philosophy for over
a decade has been that these marginally poor people should be
weaned away from welfare programs, because of what George
Gilder calls, "the moral hazard of liberalism." Gilder believes, and
writes in *Wealth and Poverty,* that welfare programs "promote the
value of being 'poor'" and "perpetuate poverty."

This is what all the talk about the "safety net" and the "truly
needy" comes down to. The Reagan theory is that only truly needy
people who cannot work should be exposed to the welfare system.
If those who can work are exposed to welfare, it is feared, they
will be drawn into the system and become permanently dependent
on it.

Many people, of course, do not agree with this theory. The remarkable thing that happened in 1981 is that this policy was enacted into law. It was enacted in many provisions of the Omnibus
Budget Reconciliation Act of 1981 in ways that few people yet ap-
preciate. Welfare programs have been fundamentally changed.
The working poor receive much less aid, in many cases nothing—
unless, of course, they stop working and become "truly needy."

There is an irony in this. The current recession is much deeper than it had been expected. One result is that many of the people who were once members of the working poor are no longer working—some because of the recession and some because of Reagan's policies. The working poor are the last hired and the first fired. If they are laid off, many in this group then become "truly needy." This presents a heady challenge for analysts. How can one determine whether a poor person who has stopped working did so because he or she now has a reduced incentive to work as a result of the 1981 cuts, or because that person lost a job as a result of the current recession?

Preliminary Prognosis

In the spring of 1981, as it became increasingly apparent that important, if not historic, changes were likely to be made in the domestic programs of the federal government, the Princeton Urban and Regional Research Center of the Woodrow Wilson School, Princeton University, began working on the design of a study of how such changes would affect state and local governments and the people they serve. The result was the initiation of a field network evaluation study, supported by a grant from the Ford Foundation and based on field evaluations in a representative sample of states and localities.

Most of the domestic spending reductions, in the fiscal year 1982 budget cuts, occurred in programs administered by state and local governments. Different state or local governments will respond to federal policy changes in different ways, depending on such factors as the government's fiscal situation, demographic conditions, and the political outlook of its decision makers. The challenge for researchers who want to study the effects of federal policy changes is first to identify them and second to explain the influence of variations in the characteristics and conditions of state and local governments.

In the complex policy setting of contemporary American federalism, no existing set of uniform data can be used for the nation as a whole to answer questions about the services reduced as a result of the Reagan administration's domestic policy changes, and about the groups affected by those changes. Federal budget data do not provide the needed information on the state and local programs and activities affected. Census data on state and local government expenditures provide only limited information on the response of states, localities, and nonprofit organizations to national policy changes. Similarly, budget documents and financial reports from state and local governments do not provide detailed, comparable information on the services and groups affected by national policy changes.

We use a field network evaluation approach as a way of collecting data and conducting analyses on a uniform basis. The field evaluations are conducted by academic economists and political scientists, all of whom are residents of the area they are studying and participate in the research on a part-time basis.

In September 1982, Transaction Books published *Reductions in U.S. Domestic Spending,* which covers the findings from the first stage of the study (October 1 to December 31, 1981, the first quarter of federal fiscal year 1982). It provides a framework for considering the changes in fiscal year 1982 and highlights some emerging indications of their effects. Five points stand out so far.

First, the cuts that were made in federal domestic spending for fiscal year 1982 affected poor people—especially the "working poor"—more than they affected the treasuries of state and local governments. Although there were exceptions, state and local governments as a rule did not replace lost federal aid for the poor with their own revenues. We refer to this behavior as "ratifying the federal cuts"—that is, allowing such benefits and programs to be reduced. By "ratify," we do not suggest that the jurisdictions necessarily approved of or willingly endorsed the cuts, but simply that they passed them on to the ultimate recipients without diverting their own dollars to make them up.

Second, other fiscal problems—the worsening recession, legal limits on spending and revenues, and the effects of earlier tax cuts—were of more immediate importance to most state and local governments than were the federal aid cuts. State and local governments were preoccupied with these problems and were largely unable to replace lost federal funds—even if they had wanted to. They frequently adopted various coping and delaying strategies to put off dealing with the fiscal year 1982 cuts for as long as they possibly could.

Third, the block grants, which tended to have high public visibility in the first year of the Reagan administration, did not result in the announced 25 percent cuts in spending in the early period, although there are indications that, over time, the cuts will have greater effects on spending and programs and will produce important institutional changes. The early budgetary effects of the block grants tended to be muted for a variety of reasons. Their full impact on political processes and institutions will take time to be felt.

Fourth, nonprofit organizations (particularly community-based organizations) appear to have been among the major victims of the cuts made in 1981. Although there is some early evidence of greater and compensatory efforts on the part of philanthropic organizations such as the United Way, other local nonprofit organizations have lost CETA workers and experienced funding cuts under the new block grant and other programs. Some of them, in fact, have gone out of business.

Fifth, the rapid pace of the process for making budget cuts in 1981 and its constantly shifting character created confusion and uncertainty on the part of state and local governments. Under these conditions, the responses of state and local governments were generally hurried and short-term accommodations. It is possible, as the Reagan administration has claimed, that its program will stimulate, in the longer run, increases in the efficiency of the domestic public sector. These and other institutional effects of the Reagan policies will be a major focus of our research in the future.

Efficiency and Accountability

The last point leads into a subject deserving of expansion. Our research has used field evaluation to study many kinds of effects of major changes in national policy—fiscal, employment, programmatic, incidence, and institutional. The category of institutional effects is the hardest to study. "Institutional effects" refers to the way in which major changes in national policy affect the machinery, processes, and politics of our governmental system. Often these effects are very subtle.

For decades, there has been a standard litany of good government—often called "goo-goo"—reforms to make government more efficient and accountable. Many people have broken lances advocating mechanisms and systems to improve the efficiency and output of particular governmental systems. One approach to "good government" is the political science approach; this is the sphere of public administration. Another more recent development has been the efforts of economists advocating reforms to enhance efficiency. Lyndon Johnson's "planning-programming-budgeting system" (PPBS) was the high point of the application of microeconomics in government. (In many ways, this is an analog to the application of macroeconomics to government in the Keynesian revolution.)

At any rate, many efforts have been made to increase governmental efficiency and accountability, despite the difficulties involved in getting public attention and winning cooperation for such efforts. But nothing makes an impression like good old-fashioned necessity—as a man once said, like the foreknowledge that you will be hanged in the morning. The hanging in this case is budget cuts—real cuts, that really will happen. Many "good government" reforms will probably now be implemented. Under the pressures of cuts, public officials have to change their ways to prove that government is worth the money—that it can get things done. One can think of such a response as "supply-side" government—that is, a new commitment in government to making domestic public bureaucracies more productive through real, and not just cosmetic, procedural changes.

Retrenchment, as stated earlier, has bubbled up throughout our governmental system—first at the local, then at the state, and now at the national level. Those of us who believe that government can be effective in dealing with social needs have no place else left to hide—or, to put it another way, no other hope that someone will bail them out.

If this kind of a persuasive change in attitude does occur, and if it affects the behavior of governmental bureaucracies in a penetrating and lasting way, it will be reflected in basic changes involving—for example—bargaining with state and local public-sector unions for "give backs"; reducing crews on sanitation trucks, police patrols, and road repair crews; and more intensive supervisory oversight of routine bureaucratic procedures for claims, taxes, grants, etc. This is what we need to be alert to. Such a change would be attributable, not just to federal aid cuts, but to a new, tougher stance toward domestic governmental agencies and programs at all levels of government.

NEW FEDERALISM OR FEUDALISM?[4]

While the nation's army of state and local officials, as well as less personally involved political scientists and economists, examine the sketchy outlines of Ronald Reagan's New Federalism last week, few quarreled with the President's professed goals. Many had long joined his call for a rollback in the overextension of the Federal Government, a more rational division of state and federal functions and the need to bring many governmental decisions closer to the people who must live with the results. The desire to get more value out of each tax dollar was warmly applauded. Declared Republican Governor James Thompson of Illinois: "It's time to give us our money back."

But there were widespread doubts, even among Reagan's most ardent supporters, that he had produced a plan that would achieve those goals. Some skeptics, most of them Democrats taking a sharply partisan view, even charged that Reagan's real motives were not as altruistic as those he set forth. They claimed that the President's aim was to rid Washington of its most troublesome domestic programs, fobbing them off on the states in the expectation that many would soon die there. Some suggested that he was trying especially to get the problems of the poor off Washington's back.

New York City's Democratic Mayor Ed Koch termed the Reagan plan "a con job, a snare and a delusion, a steal by the Feds," adding, "I don't think he understands the impact of what he is

⁴ Article from *Time*. 119:19–20. F. 8, '82. Reprinted by permission from TIME. Copyright 1982 Time Inc. All rights reserved.

doing." New York's Democratic Governor Hugh Carey contended that the New Federalism is really "a new feudalism," which will pit states against each other and cities against their state capitals as all struggle anew for a fair share of dwindling federal funds or jockey to protect their own economic interests. In the same vein, Democratic Governor Jerry Brown of California warned that the 50 states might become "competing colonies." West Virginia's Democratic Governor Jay Rockefeller charged that Reagan was "dumping onto the states what he doesn't want to face up to himself."

While applauding the push for some decentralization, Political Scientist Paul Peterson, chairman of the Committee on Public Policy Studies at the University of Chicago, wondered about Reagan's intent. "If your overall purpose is to reduce benefits to the needy without appearing to do so," he said, "then the answer is to shift responsibility for serving the needy to state and local governments."

Even those who did not question the President's motives found it difficult to defend his particular reshuffling of federal and state roles. Academic theoreticians and practical politicians alike see a need for a federal hand in helping the poor, since their problems are often created by national economic conditions. Only a federal presence can apply pressure to hold down the inequities stemming from a state's relative inability or unwillingness to deal fairly with the problem. States and cities, on the other hand, can more effectively make decisions on how to provide such basic public services as schools, roads, water, sewage and transit systems.

Reagan's proposed realignment would indeed eventually free Washington from its current responsibility to help states and cities improve their traditional local services. But his more immediate "swap" of programs, which would go into effect in October 1983, would also toss two of the Federal Government's largest, most difficult and most controversial welfare services, food stamps and Aid to Families with Dependent Children, back to the states. In this exchange, Washington would take over full funding and operation of Medicaid, a program that supplies health care to many of the same people helped by the other two services. The primary rationale seems to be a matter of political convenience. The Administration's dubious projection of AFDC and food stamp costs slightly exceeds that of Medicaid—and without the enticement of getting out from under the faster-growing Medicaid program, the states obviously would never agree to take on the other two burdens. At issue in the swap are these programs:

AFDC. The nation's basic welfare program, it provided benefits to 11.1 million individuals last year at a cost of $6.9 billion to the Federal Government and $5.89 billion to the states. Each state is free to set its own level of benefits, which range from $96 a month for a family of three in Mississippi to more than $200 for a similar family in New York. The Federal Government matches what the states decide to pay. The program already is basically administered by state and local governments, with Washington bearing half of these administrative costs.

FOOD STAMPS. This program has 21.7 million recipients, whose eligibility is determined under regulations from Washington. The cost last year was $11.4 billion, with the Federal Government picking up all of the tab. While the stamps are distributed by state and county officials, the program is mainly a federal one.

MEDICAID. The program, which provides medical care for the poor (unlike Medicare, which serves the elderly, it has no age requirement), aided some 22 million people last year at a cost of $30.5 billion. The Federal Government assumes about 55 percent of the total cost, which has been growing at nearly 15 percent annually, far above the inflation rate. The states have been free to provide optional services, such as eyeglasses and prescription drugs, with Washington sharing this cost. Benefits and eligibility standards vary from state to state. In the proposed federal takeover, it is unclear how Washington would accommodate these differences.

Understandably, the proposed shift of programs sent state finance officials scurrying off to their computers to determine just how they would fare in dollars. And while presidential aides tried, unpersuasively, to assure Governors that there would be no state winners or losers when, and if, the swap is approved by Congress, the estimated disparities sometimes were large. Officials in Ohio, who already face a $1 billion state budget deficit, figured the state would lose perhaps $400 million in the exchange. Florida estimates its loss at $455 million. Tennessee at $206.8 million, West

Virginia at $110 million, Minnesota, on the other hand, expects to gain about $90 million from the swap, while New York's gain could go as high as $1.3 billion, if Washington picks up the state's optional payments, which seems unlikely.

White House estimates, which predict a much better fate for the states than local officials do, foresee the states emerging with a net combined gain of more than $2.5 billion. Obviously, all such projections are murky, with various officials making different assumptions about just what would happen. "The numbers thrown around by the President look suspicious," contends Economics Professor Bernard Weinstein of the University of Texas. "State and local governments will get the shaft as well as the shift."

The more basic issue, as Vermont's Republican Governor Richard Snelling views it, is that "this is not a numbers game, but a question of how people will be served." Most critics of the swap see a great danger that once federal funding of AFDC and food stamps ends, many states will deliberately keep such benefits low in the expectation that the poor will move to states where benefits are higher. Contends Felix Rohatyn, a New York financial expert who has advised states and cities on their money problems: "All poverty programs should be funded by the Federal Government; otherwise, states are going to compete by driving poor people into other states." To Princeton University's Richard P. Nathan, a professor of public affairs, the plan "sets up all the wrong incentives."

While some sociologists fear the federal withdrawal could spur a renewed wave of migration of the needy from the South to Northern and Western states, where benefits are comparatively generous, Atlanta Mayor Andrew Young worries about even shorter flights. "If Alabama decides to be irresponsible," he says, "Atlanta will be flooded with poor people."

The Administration's rebuttal is that voting rights gains among blacks and reapportionment of state legislatures have given the poor greater political clout, making it less likely that legislatures will act harshly to lower current welfare and food stamp benefits. Political Scientist William K. Muir at the University of California in Berkeley agrees. "Thirty years ago, you had a political system rigged against the poor and the black. But by and large, that has been cured. It's very rare to see a diminution of the franchise once it has been obtained."

Reagan's decision to give up AFDC and food stamp programs, which he has criticized as being vastly abused, while retaining Medicaid, in which abuses are more likely to be committed by doctors who overtreat and overprescribe than by the indigent ill, angers some state officials. Says Gerald M. Thornton, director of social services for North Carolina's Forsyth County: "He wants to take Medicaid, a respectable program, and give us food stamps, a program that's so unpopular that a person who gets stamps might as well be wearing tattoos. That's like getting a gift of garbage."

Vermont's Snelling, who is chairman of the National Governors Association, notes that the Governors have long sought a reexamination of the many federal aid programs, but have specifically opposed giving welfare responsibilities back to the states. To the contrary, they have asked the Federal Government to operate and fund all income-maintenance programs, while seeking full control of many of the road-building and similar capital construction projects. Nevertheless, Snelling welcomes the President's initiative. "There's enough federalism in his proposal, coupled with his intention to consult with us, for us to start talking."

Many state officials worry even more about whether Reagan's plan to temporarily fund 43 other programs with a $28 billion trust fund will prove adequate. Among the programs that would be affected: grants for airports, noninterstate highways, mass transit, water and sewer systems, community development, vocational education, child abuse, child nutrition, migrant health clinics, locating runaway youths and crime prevention.

Adding up his own numbers, Governor Rockefeller estimates this fund will fall at least $19 billion short of keeping the programs going at their current levels. After this fund is scheduled to be phased out in 1991, Reagan's invitation to the states to replace the federal money by passing higher excise taxes* to keep the programs going, or to kill the programs, meets with little en-

---

*An excise tax differs little from a sales tax except that it applies to a specific product rather than being levied as a fixed percentage on a broad range of products. Excise taxes on liquor and tobacco are often called "sin taxes."

thusiasm, even though he has offered to repeal most current federal excise taxes on gasoline, tobacco and alcohol at that time.

Many states are financially strapped and find it difficult politically to seek more tax hikes. The states already levy excise taxes at varying rates. Receipts for such taxes, which disproportionately hurt low-income earners, show that the states are taking in more money from cigarettes and gasoline than Washington does.

Moreover, the grass-roots anti-tax movement of the past few years has put tight limits on tax increases in many states. Another limitation on state fund raising: the closer an elected official is to the electorate, the harder it is for him to raise taxes and survive. Republican Paul Gillmor, president of the Ohio state senate, flatly predicts that any programs turned over to Ohio with insufficient funding "will simply be terminated," which may well be what the Administration has in mind.

The likelihood that the financially pressed states and cities are better equipped to administer many federal aid programs than Washington's more distant bureaucrats is also challenged by some experts. Contends Michael Luger, assistant professor of public policy studies at Duke University: "Certain states are managed better than others, but, typically, the Federal Government has much better trained personnel and better managers." It also has many more of them at much higher salaries, which is part of the problem. Though states have their own waste and corruption problems, the general competence of their officials seems to be growing.

For all its obvious faults and great uncertainties, Ronald Reagan's New Federalism proposals were generally welcomed as the start of an overdue and refreshing national dialogue. The debate may be a long one, but it is almost certain to be worthwhile.

EDITOR'S INTRODUCTION

There's no question that where Federal regulation of industry is concerned, the Reagan administration's sympathies lie with the regulated, not with the regulators. In an attempt to return to the practices of an earlier age, the Reagan administration has proposed to allow corporations to regulate themselves rather than maintaining the regulatory powers of the Federal government.

In the overall scheme of Reaganomics, deregulation is supposed to aid industrial productivity, because the resources formerly devoted to complying with regulations can now be used for profit-making activities, which will in turn pave the way to economic prosperity.

The Reagan people have been able to bring about much deregulation without changing the law. They have simply assigned fewer people to enforce the codes that are already on the books. When manpower in the regulatory agencies decreases, strong enforcement becomes impossible.

David L. Barnett, reporting for the *U.S. News & World Report,* shows how Reagan has used budget cuts, firings and the appointments of tough new bosses to curb the strength of regulatory agencies. He quotes Robert W. Hartman, a Brookings Institution senior fellow and an expert on government organization who explains the Reagan administration's "use of personnel policy to make broad policy without getting Congress to change the law. In the regulatory agencies, for instance, with fewer people to enforce regulations and laws, it means weaker enforcement and it is being done consciously."

In an article from *The Nation,* Fred J. Cook, author of *The Great Energy Scam: Private Billions vs. Public Good,* says that the oil industry is an important benefactor of deregulation. He shows how deregulation of oil and gas prices will enable oil companies to dominate the energy market and charge artificially high prices for oil and gas.

According to Mark Green, president of the Democracy Project, a public policy institute, deregulation has been a failure. Writing in *The New Republic,* Green shows how a combination of public backlash against aspects of the deregulatory effort, legislative rejections, and lost court cases have blocked the deregulation effort.

The fourth article in this section deals with the Administration's proposals for the transfer to the states of social programs that have formerly been the responsibility of the Federal government. In *Society,* Sar A. Levitan, research professor of economics and director of the Center for Social Policy Studies at the George Washington University, says the Federal government and the states must accept equal responsibility for social programs. In Levitan's view, the states may have too little responsibility now, but they should not be given too much responsibility in the future or the system will merely create a different type of inequity.

James Nathan Miller, an editor of *Reader's Digest,* thinks the battle over deregulation has just begun. In Miller's view, Reagan's appointees have given industry permission to ride roughshod over the environment and consumer well being. Miller, like Green, thinks that deregulation won't work, but he also feels that "the environmental structure . . . is badly damaged and will require time to repair."

A WAR REAGAN'S WINNING: TAMING THE BUREAUCRACY[1]

The White House has put such a squeeze on government workers that President Reagan is on his way to a goal that has eluded Presidents for decades: Getting a firm rein on federal civil servants. "The President has been more successful in bring the bureaucracy under control than any other President," declares White House personnel chief E. Pendleton James.

[1] Magazine article by David L. Barnett. Reprinted from *U.S. News & World Report* 92:26–27. Ap. 5, '82. Copyright 1982, U.S. News & World Report, Inc.

A career employee admits frustration: "They've about got us in a straitjacket. The Reaganites won't listen to anybody who was here before the inauguration. They are not only determined to rediscover the wheel, they want it rediscovered to their rigid specifications—even if it turns out to be square."

The battle to make nonpostal civil servants toe Reagan's philosophical line has been raging from the day the new team took office in January, 1981. Behind the skirmishing is the suspicion by Reagan officials that unsympathetic careerists among the 2.7 million federal workers would try to sabotage the President's program by using delaying tactics or by undermining orders of political appointees.

That complaint is not unique to the Reagan administration. President Harry Truman, as he left office in 1953, predicted that his successsor, Dwight Eisenhower, would sit in the Oval Office and say, "'Do this. Do that.' And nothing will happen." Most successors have made much the same complaint.

To make things happen the way Reagan wants them to, the White House has employed three major devices:

Sharp funding cuts and rule changes that starve policies that some bureaucrats and their congressional allies have promoted for years.

Personnel firings—reductions of some 43,000 nondefense jobs in 1981, with 75,000 more expected this year—that make civil servants fear to buck policies or even to offer alternatives. James says fear of getting fired has "big motivating power."

Tight White House monitoring of appointees to the top 400 subcabinet posts to make sure they remain faithful to Reagan positions.

One measure of how well Reagan has mastered the bureaucracy: In some cases it has been possible to slow funding of programs that the President's men want to cut, despite the wishes of Congress.

A prime example is housing for the elderly and the handicapped. The subsidized projects have had the enthusiastic support of many in government who argue that they have been needed and well maintained—unlike the deteriorating and crime-ridden public-housing projects for families. Nevertheless, the Department of

Housing and Urban Development, by setting strict deadlines to begin construction, is expected to knock out 1,600 units, one fourth of the new starts approved by Congress.

Shaking up—and some critics say intimidating—the civil servants has not been without risks for the Reagan administration. Many of the most experienced government workers have departed, rather than face more war in the bureaucratic trenches. In the past year, about half the top civil servants have taken retirement in the first year they were eligible—some at age 50 after 30 years of service. In 1979, the ratio was less than one third.

At the Consumer Product Safety Commission, so many have headed for the exits that personnel strength is already below the level set for next year. Similar shortages are developing at the Environmental Protection Agency, the Federal Trade Commission and the Interstate Commerce Commission.

Fewer Watchdogs

Says Robert W. Hartman, a Brookings Institution senior fellow and an expert on government organization: "The most unique operation is the use of personnel policy to make broad policy without getting Congress to change the law. In the regulatory agencies, for instance, with fewer people to enforce regulations and laws, it means weaker enforcement, and it is being done consciously."

The reason for freezing out some bureaucrats, says a Reagan appointee in the Labor Department, is simple: "I can't trust advice from a dedicated government activist when we're trying to curb programs."

Edwin Meese III, counselor to the President, figures that 10 to 20 percent of the bureaucrats will always oppose what the administration wants and should be isolated; another 10 to 20 percent "have been waiting for someone like the President to come along," and the rest will do what they are told.

Problems at the Small Business Administration illustrate how conflicts between political appointees and civil servants can escalate. A feud started when SBA chief Michael Cardenas, a Reagan appointee, insisted that he personally approve many routine decisions made previously at the local or regional level. As decisions began piling up in Washington, some careerists began informing members of Congress when a pending decision involving a constituent was tied up awaiting action by Cardenas.

Cardenas countered with a handwritten memo to department heads: "Just a word of caution. Anytime I receive a call saying I have things on my desk for signature . . . I am obtaining names from the caller. Personnel files will be documented, and action will be taken accordingly." The administration finally decided in February to remove Cardenas. The bureaucrats considered it one of their few victories in this administration.

Adding to the friction in federal agencies is the open distrust of bureaucrats shown by Donald Devine, the Reagan-appointed director of the Office of Personnel Management, which runs the civil-service system. Devine had security doors installed to block off the agency's executive suite from the bureaucrats. He recently sent letters on OPM stationery to his fellow Maryland conservatives citing his achievements in his battles with the federal workers, including his attempt to eliminate abortion coverage from government employees' medical plans—an effort the courts blocked.

Bureaucrats really have two bosses—the President and Congress. Sometimes politicians and careerists differ on what Congress meant. That was the issue in a recent dispute at the Justice Department. More than 200 lawyers and other employees protested a decision to support tax breaks to private schools that discriminate.

At a closed-door meeting of Assistant Atty. Gen. William Bradford Reynolds and the protesting government lawyers, the argument got so heated that one lawyer told Reynolds: "There's an overall mistrust of you to the point where you are rapidly becoming a general without an army." Reynolds's answer: "Then I'll have to find myself a new army." Justice Department lawyers were invited to leave the government if they disagreed with Reagan's policies, but so far there have been few reports of such resignations.

Reagan appointees have on occasion backed down when faced with evidence of clear orders from Congress. Example: some regulations put on the White House hit list last August are still on the books, not because bureaucrats sabotaged the deregulation program but because the political appointees conceded that the regulations are specifically mandated by statutes.

Self-inflicted Wound

One of the biggest episodes in the bureaucratic warfare has been the ketchup caper. Last October, the Department of Agriculture listed ketchup as a substitute for a vegetable in school lunches. President Reagan pulled back the regulation, saying, "Somebody got overambitious in the bureaucracy." But it was the President's own bureaucracy, not the one he inherited from the Democratic administration. Those responsible were Reagan appointees.

Still, there is no doubt that there are career officials who are unsympathetic with Reagan policies. Explains a 12-year veteran of the civil service: "I've spent the best years of my life working on ways to get training for the unemployed so they can hold jobs. Now, most of the programs are being junked, and I am considered an enemy of the people who has done nothing but waste taxpayers' money. I'm frustrated and angry."

For Reagan supporters, a crackdown on dissident careerists is considered essential to make sure that the President's programs get a fair chance. Opponents argue that such a tough approach could freeze the flow of new ideas, opinions and research going to policymakers.

Robert Buford, director of the Bureau of Land Management, told workers that "it is inappropriate for a bureau employee to express opinions . . . if they differ from the administration position." Analysts at the Environmental Protection Agency were warned that Administrator Anne Gorsuch is "fed up" with research that undermines administration proposals.

For all the disputes, Reagan is succeeding where other Presidents failed: He is turning the huge federal bureaucracy against itself to achieve his goal of curbing the size and influence of the Washington establishment.

BIG OIL'S STAKE IN DEREGULATION[2]

The Energy Establishment—a close network of the big oil companies, the large banks and the major pipeline companies— has thrown its support behind President Reagan's bill decontrolling all natural gas prices. Restore the "free market," its public relations organs tell the public, and America will enter a new era of low prices and abundant supplies.

One such champion of justice for the consumer is C. C. Garvin Jr., chairman of the board of Exxon, the struggling oil giant which in the worst of quarters earns an average profit of a mere $1 billion. Garvin led off the spring issue of *The Lamp,* the magazine that goes to every Exxon stockholder, with a two-page essay entitled "The Illogic of Natural Gas Price Controls." He wrote:

For almost thirty years now, a commodity of great value to individual consumers and to entire industries has been regulated at prices below those of competitive fuels [meaning oil]. It makes little sense that this should continue indefinitely.

Instead, *"all"* (Garvin's emphasis) natural gas should be allowed "to achieve market levels during the next few years." According to Garvin, this upward price achievement would encourage the search for new energy supplies and discourage the improvident from wasting precious fuel.

"Experience and logic have shown that we are wise to remove oil price controls," he concluded, predicting the same beneficial results from natural gas decontrol.

Actually, the oil companies support the Reagan proposal because it will enable them to extract billions of dollars from consumers and will give the Energy Establishment a monopoly. Decontrol will push up natural gas prices and drive out independent producers, leaving Big Oil and its allies to roll like spring colts in the deep green. More than $50 billion in additional annual revenues—possibly as much as $100 billion—will be theirs if Reagan's bill passes.

    [2] Magazine article by Fred J. Cook, author of *The Great Energy Scam: Private Billions vs. Public Good.* *The Nation.* 236:630–632. My. 21, '83. Copyright 1983 The Nation Magazine, The Nation Associates, Inc.

To understand the dominance the Energy Establishment now exercises over the nation's natural gas market, one could do no better than to study the brief filed on August 26, 1982, with the Federal Energy Regulatory Commission (F.E.R.C.) by the New England Community Action Program Directors Association, the Consumers' Education and Protection Association, the Office of Consumers' Council for the State of Ohio and the Public Advocate Division of the Public Service Commission of West Virginia.

Relying on evidence gathered by the Federal Power Commission, the brief shows that in the late 1960s and early 1970s, the largest U.S. oil companies either acquired or entered into partnership with the leading gas pipeline companies. As the brief declares, "The fact that all major interstate pipelines have producing affiliates is one of the critical factors undermining the potential for competitive interplay in the gas producer market."

The same web of companies that dominates the interstate gas market also controls the key intrastate market. The Natural Gas Act of 1938, which kept prices stable until the 1970s, only regulated interstate prices. Producers took advantage of this opening and raised prices in the intrastate market. In the bitter winter of 1976–77, they withheld their gas from the interstate market, creating a scarcity and throwing 2 million people out of work in the Midwest. The effect of this power play was to drive up interstate prices. In 1978, Congress passed the Natural Gas Policy Act (NGPA), which phases out controls on "new gas" by the end of 1985. "Old gas" (gas from wells in production before the act was passed) was not decontrolled, but the act brought the Energy Establishment a step closer to its goal of completely unregulated prices.

The brief filed with the F.E.R.C. gives a lineup of the companies behind this power play. An eleven-page table lists producers who own intrastate pipeline companies that also sell on the interstate market. According of the brief:

Such majors as Exxon (Monterey Pipeline), Continental Oil, Texaco and Phillips Petroleum have major intrastate pipeline networks. One of the practices used by the major producers during the 1970s was to bid up prices in the intrastate market for the purchases for their intrastate pipeline system, then use these prices as evidence before the F.P.C. [Federal

Power Commission] of going prices levels in the intrastate market that had to be met to attract gas for emergency sales in the interstate market [a reference to the situation in 1976–77, when cold weather created an exceptionally high demand for gas].

Another table shows numerous direct links between producers and pipeline companies—in this instance, companies involved in offshore leasing operations. In almost every case, the oil company was a partner of one or more of the major pipeline firms. For example, Atlantic-Richfield held ninety-four leases in partnership with other major oil firms and two pipeline companies, Tenneco and El Paso. Tenneco was a partner of Cities Service in seven of its leases. Continental held eight leases in partnership with Tenneco and two with Southern Natural, which was also a partner of Phillips Petroleum, Getty, Amoco and Kerr-McGee.

The oil and pipeline companies also formed "interlocks" with large banks; more than eighty directors of the banks served as directors of two or more oil companies. As a table in the brief shows:

On Exxon's board, there were members from Chase Manhattan, Citibank, and the First National Bank of Chicago. On Mobil's board, there were members from Citibank (also Exxon), First National Bank of Boston, and Bankers Trust. Standard of Indiana (Amoco) had members on its board from Chase Manhattan (also Exxon), First National Bank of Chicago, Continental Illinois, Harris Trust and American National Bank (Chicago).

These links between Big Oil and Big Money, the brief says, "raise serious questions about competitive performance. Would these financial institutions freely provide capital to an existing or potential competitor if the capital would adversely affect the firms in which the banks have an interest?"

Certainly the banking-oil interlocks put billions of dollars at the disposal of the oil companies. Morgan Guaranty Trust, for example, had director interlocks with Louisiana Land and Exploration, Belco Petroleum, Texas Gulf Sulphur (in which it also held a substantial financial interest), Continental Oil, Cities Service, Atlantic-Richfield and Columbia Gas System. The bank also had large holdings in Texas Eastern Transmission, Panhandle Eastern Pipeline and numerous gas distribution utilities. In addition to its connections with Exxon and Amoco, Chase Manhattan owned 5.6 percent of the common stock of Panhandle Eastern Pipeline. Other banks mentioned in the brief had similar interlocking ties with various producing and transporting companies.

David Schwartz, assistant chief at the Office of Economics in the Federal Power Commission (which was abolished in 1978, when its powers were transferred to the new Department of Energy), explained the significance of what he called an "extensive web" of influence, in testimony before a House committee on March 21, 1975:

The evidence presented on both the buying side and the selling side of the natural gas producer market reflects serious market imperfections that are so all-pervasive that they render competition unworkable. The various institutional arrangements reflecting interdependence and commonality of interests preclude rivalry and competitive interplay. The implications for competition and new entry, as well as reasonable prices, are clear in that the public interest cannot be served by deregulation in a market manifesting these oligopolistic characteristics.

The oligopoly dominated the natural gas market in the 1970s and drove up unregulated intrastate prices from 63 cents per thousand cubic feet in 1972 to $1.40 per thousand cubic feet in 1975. In that same period, the controlled price of interstate gas rose from 29 cents to 57 cents. The oligopoly members' contempt for the national interest was evident when they capped their wells in 1976 and 1977. The producers got part of what they wanted in the 1978 NGPA—the provision for gradual decontrol of new gas.

Now the Energy Establishment is seeking to finish the job at a time of skyrocketing prices and a natural gas glut, which, according to free-market teachings, should have brought prices down, but did not. Contrary to their claims, Big Oil and its partners are not pushing for complete decontrol because it would result in more and cheaper gas. Rather, as an exhaustive study by the Consumer Federation of America recently concluded, "Just twenty natural gas producers stand to gain a $68.3 billion 'windfall' from their sales of old gas to only fifteen interstate pipelines for the period 1983–1990."

The C.F.A. report, which draws on figures compiled by the American Petroleum Institute, an industry group, names the following companies as the prime beneficiaries of old gas decontrol:

Mobil, Exxon, Texaco, Gulf, Shell, Tenneco, Standard Oil of Indiana (Amoco), Standard Oil of California (Chevron), Phillips Petroleum, Atlantic-Richfield, Getty, Cities Service, Union, Superior, Sun, El Paso, Conoco, Penzoil, Marathon and Columbia.

These corporations own most of the country's supply of old gas. Consumer Federation researchers found that they had supplied 72.3 percent of all such gas that flowed through the pipelines in 1982. The five leaders were Mobil, with 383.1 billion cubic feet selling for $532.5 million; Exxon, 365.4 billion cubic feet, $514.4 million; Texaco, 355.3 billion cubic feet, $427.4 million; Gulf, 332.6 billion cubic feet, $193.9 million; Shell, 319.7 billion cubic feet, $451.1 million. Gulf, tied to contracts negotiated years ago, was the only company that was hurting; it received an average of only 58 cents per thousand cubic feet, compared with the national price of $1.26 per thousand cubic feet.

Although the other major oil companies are not stuck with such a large number of low-cost contracts, many are complaining. Phillips Petroleum, for example, claims that it is selling some gas from its Texas fields for 19.7 cents per thousand cubic feet under long-term contracts, and Texaco moans that it received an average of only 98 cents per thousand cubic feet for its 1980 production. Given those figures, it is not hard to grasp the benefits to the oligopolists from the Reagan bill, since it has a "market out" clause that would enable them to terminate old gas contracts, letting prices zoom to the average market rate, which was $2.53 per thousand cubic feet in the fall of 1982.

Many independent gas producers contend that such windfalls for the wealthiest companies would drive hundreds of smaller firms out of business. Robert A. Hefner 3d, head of The GHK Companies in Oklahoma City, spokesman for the Independent Gas Producers Committee and a harsh critic of decontrol, told Representative Philip Sharp's fossil and synthetic fuels subcommittee on March 24:

The proposal crafted by the Department of Energy would be a disaster for both current producers and users of natural gas. It is a no-win proposition for everyone but the major oil companies. It is a bill which robs consumers of the benefit of low cost, old gas supplies, robs independent producers of essential incentives to drill for new reserves and robs our country of the chance to displace higher cost foreign oil with lower cost domestic gas.

Hefner charged that the bill, in time, "would confer a $100 billion windfall on the major oil companies," and he added this warning: "If independent producers are driven out of business, the same multinational companies that already own America's oil, uranium and coal supplies will soon dominate the ownership of newly discovered gas reserves as well."

There is much evidence to support Hefner's prediction. Consider the effects of the "backdoor decontrol" measures introduced by the F.E.R.C. in 1982, which increased gas prices to consumers by 25 to 50 percent, lowered demand and discouraged exploration. The experience of one independent producer, Mesa Petroleum, was typical. According to company president T. Boone Pickens Jr., in an interview broadcast on public television in January, Mesa's drillers discovered a reservoir capable of producing 20 billion cubic feet of gas a day, after drilling 26,000 feet in Oklahoma's Anadarko Basin. But this find proved valueless: Mesa couldn't get a single pipeline company to transport the gas because there was no demand for it.

In November 1981, I called the Department of Energy for information about a phenomenon that seemed inexplicable to me. For the past two years, homeowners had been converting from No. 2 fuel oil to natural gas for heating, at a rate of 400,000 a year. Yet natural gas consumption had dropped. According to the department's own figures, consumption fell 7 percent in 1979, to 19.5 trillion cubic feet—and it fell again in 1980, to 18.7 trillion cubic feet.

A spokesman for the department explained that natural gas consumption had declined in 1979 and 1980 because prices were *too high*. He said that when No. 6 residual oil became cheaper than gas, many large-volume consumers converted with the flip of a switch, since their boilers were capable of burning either fuel.

Now, two years later, with natural gas prices going berserk, the industry is confronted with a crisis of dwindling markets and shrinking demand. Numerous witnesses before the Sharp subcommittee testified that the low volume of sales—not a shortage of gas—was the industry's most critical problem. The Energy Establishment has been driving up prices in an effort to make natural gas "competitive" with oil. But the oligopolists' definition of "competitive" stands English on its head. They want natural gas to cost as much as oil—or more. Then the American consumer would have no competing fuels to choose between. The world would belong to Big Oil, the czar of the marketplace. Big Oil, and Big Oil alone, would determine all energy costs—and the public be damned.

THE GANG THAT CAN'T DEREGULATE[3]

All Reaganomics is divided into four parts, three of which (tax cuts, budget cuts, and tight money) we have heard much about. But until the Environmental Protection Agency began self-immolating, little attention was paid to the fourth part: deregulation. This was certainly not for the Administration's lack of trying. President Reagan entered the White House determined, among other things, to overhaul all those regulatory agencies he had denounced for three decades as a threat to personal freedom and economic growth. David Stockman's famous "Economic Dunkirk" memo urged "a dramatic, substantial recision of the regulatory burden"; within 48 hours of taking the oath of office, Reagan created the Presidential Task Force on Regulatory Relief, chaired by Vice President George Bush; a week later, the task force suspended nearly two hundred "midnight regulations" proposed late in the Carter Administration; and on February 17 the President issued an executive order requiring that proposed regulations pass a cost-benefit test. In late 1981, *The Washington Post* ran a World War II size headline: U.S. DISMANTLING CONSUMER PROGRAMS.

But two years after its opening burst, Reagan's deregulatory jihad must be judged a short-term success and long-term failure.

[3] Magazine article by Mark Green, president of the Democracy Project, a public policy institute. *New Republic*. 188:14–17. Mr. 21, '83. Reprinted by permission of The New Republic. © 1983 The New Republic, Inc.

There is no question that the Administration has slowed the advance of federal regulation by making antiregulatory appointments, shrinking regulatory agency budgets, reducing information disclosure, weakening enforcement, and simply refusing to propose or approve new pending regulations. At the same time, however, the Administration has failed to significantly deregulate Washington. This is the nearly unanimous conclusion on both sides in the regulatory debate. "The Administration has fumbled the ball," says James Carty, regulatory affairs director of the National Association of Manufacturers. "They've blown it." George Eads of the Rand Corporation says, "They have stopped issuing and enforcing regulations, but they haven't attacked the basis for regulation." "They hurt their cause," adds Marvin Kosters of the American Enterprise Institute. And Simon Lazarus III, who worked on regulatory issues in Jimmy Carter's White House, says, "It's incredible that with a Republican Senate, business groups up in arms, and a committed Administration, they've achieved so little."

What went wrong? Administration deregulators, as so many of Reagan's top appointments, overreached and produced a backlash that now hamstrings them in the agencies, in the courts, and in Congress.

The reaction began well before the troubles at E.P.A., with symbols such as the Task Force on Regulatory Relief, which confessed in its title that its goal was to help business, not consumers. And the White House's selection of appointees known for hostility to the purpose of their agencies approached the contemptuous. Armand Hammer, head of Hooker Chemical's parent corporation, was named to head a Presidential advisory committee on cancer. John McKetta, a lobbyist against the Clean Air Act, served on an interagency Acid Preparation Task Force, despite his observation that "grass and trees in my backyard" pollute more than his car. Other appointees have contended that ketchup is a vegetable and that bribery in trucking is simply the free market at work. At the Federal Trade Commission, chairman James Miller III said that "imperfect products should be available because consumers have different preferences for defect avoidance"—which translated from the original Darwin means that poorer consumers should be allowed to buy dangerous products since they can't afford better in a free market. One of Miller's economists recently recommended against recalling six thousand defective survival suits, arguing that the families of victims should instead sue for compensation. A disbelieving Representative Al Gore said: "Some screwball thought market forces could be defined as lawsuits by widows and orphans."

Anne Burford at E.P.A., Nancy Steorts at the Consumer Product Safety Commission, and John Shad at the Securities and Exchange Commission also made serious tactical mistakes from the start. Burford and Steorts showed open contempt for professionals in their agencies. One of Steorts's first acts was to spend almost $10,000 to decorate her office at the same time her agency received a 25 percent budget cut. Shad, a major fundraiser for Reagan on Wall Street, gave a $1,000 campaign contribution to New York Senator Alfonse D'Amato after D'Amato became chairman of the subcommittee overseeing the S.E.C. Then he opposed the prosecution of Citibank for its alleged evasion of foreign tax and currency laws, arguing that management never said it would act with honesty and integrity, so it didn't have to disclose breaches of those standards. The S.E.C.'s enforcement chief, John Fedders, meanwhile, has announced a policy of not going after fraudulent practices that don't "materially" affect the company's financial performance.

Reagan appointees obviously misread the 1980 election as a mandate for wholesale regulatory dismantling, but poll results indicate fundamental support for consumer and environmental regulation. A recent Harris survey indicates that 88 percent of Americans want the Clean Air Act kept intact or strengthened. When people were asked if they would still want the act enforced if jobs were threatened, they said yes by a margin of 78 percent to 17 percent. *Public Opinion* magazine found that only 9 percent of the public wants worker-safety regulations reduced, 32 percent wants them as they are, and 59 percent wants them strengthened.

Whatever its periodic errors or excesses, federal environmental and consumer regulation has worked, and the regulation is needed. Product safety standards on cribs and bottle caps have cut infant deaths from crib strangulation and ingestion of poisons or pills by 50 percent. The Clean Air Act has created 200,000 jobs and has provided $21.4 billion worth of economic and health benefits annually. Federal auto and traffic regulations have prevented approximately 100,000 deaths from automobile accidents. Reaganite anecdotes about the evils of big government are less effective following word that Oraflex, approved by the Food and Drug Administration as part of its expedited new drug approval process, has been associated with 61 deaths in Great Britain.

The antideregulation backlash has now been joined by Republicans and business people as well as consumer and environmental activists. The National Wildlife Federation, two-thirds of whose members voted for Reagan, publicly urged that he fire Interior Secretary James Watt. Exxon and Bacardi, companies that spent large sums meeting E.P.A. water standards, expressed annoyance when those standards were eased—"rewarding companies that failed to comply," one businessman said. An early OSHA proposal to do away with labeling of hazardous work-place chemicals upset chemical industry lobbyists who feared they soon would be facing "fifty little E.P.A.s and OSHAs" in the states. When E.P.A. suffered extensive budget cuts, impairing its ability to develop timely and intelligent regulations, Geraldine V. Cox of the Chemical Manufacturers Association complained that "if E.P.A. can't operate, we can't either."

The backlash now is limiting President Reagan's declared goal of reducing the level of regulation—administratively, judicially, and legislatively. The regulatory agencies themselves are pulling back from announced changes. Former Health and Human Services Secretary Richard Schweiker planned to lower requirements for nursing home certification and inspection, but after Republican Senator John Heinz announced the proposal had "just about zero support," Schweiker withdrew it. Thorne Auchter at OSHA announced that safety inspectors' promotion chances would be partly based on employers' evaluations, which of course could make inspectors more obsequious than observant. Labor complained, and the policy ended. After Interior Secretary James Watt began oil and gas leasing in a New Mexico wilderness area in late 1981, public opposition caused the House Interior Committee to make him stop.

The most frequent about-faces have occurred at E.P.A. Without hearings or public comment, the agency announced in February 1982 that it was suspending a ban on liquid wastes in landfills. There was an immediate public and Congressional revolt, which included Representative Guy Molinari, a conservative Republican from New York City. "Even as we meet here," he declared at an E.P.A. hearing, "the trucks are rolling into nine hundred landfills all over America carrying a deadly legacy that our children and our grandchildren will have no choice but to accept." Within three weeks E.P.A. reinstated the ban. Also in February 1982, the agency proposed to abolish or weaken limits on the amount of lead in gasoline; this would increase the amount of lead in the air, which is especially dangerous to children. Six months later, E.P.A. was forced to reverse itself, and proposed to strengthen the standard. After balking for months, the agency issued regulations that schools be inspected for loose asbestos and that toxic waste facility operators have the financial resources to safely maintain a site after it has been closed.

In the Courts the Administration has suffered a series of setbacks because its zealous antiregulators ignored legal standards. In April 1981 OSHA tried to get the Supreme Court to stop considering a case involving cotton dust standards for textile workers. The Administration wanted to subject the standards to cost-benefit analysis, but the Court ruled that it wasn't legal. Justice William Brennan declared that the health of workers outweighs "all other considerations" and that Congress intended compliance to be "part of the cost of doing business." In another major test case, the State Farm Mutual Insurance Company sued Reagan's National Highway Traffic Safety Administration for abolishing the passive restraint (or so-called "air bag") rule. Judge Abner Mikva, writing for a unanimous U.S. Court of Appeals for the District of Columbia, called N.H.T.S.A.'s action "arbitrary and unlawful." He said that the agency "seems to conclude that because some technology will not meet the passive restraint standard, it need not mandate compliance by technology that will. The absurdity of this Orwellian reasoning is obvious." N.H.T.S.A. has appealed to the Supreme Court.

Recently Public Citizen and other groups sued the Food and Drug Administration, claiming that it had gutted infant formula regulations because of pressure from industry. Plaintiffs disclosed an F.D.A. memorandum in which an agency attorney admitted that the regulations were so altered as to be "hardly recognizable," and that "the agency would probably lose a court challenge"; an F.D.A. spokesman later confirmed that the regulations were extensively rewritten to satisfy industry complaints.

Of all the agencies, E.P.A. has the worst judicial record. It has lost at least four major cases since Anne Burford became Administrator, three times to the National Resources Defense Fund alone. For example, in June 1982, the U.S. Court of Appeals in Philadelphia said the agency had acted illegally when it suspended federal rules on toxic waste discharges, and ordered the regulation retroactively reinstituted. The next month, the Court of Appeals in the District of Columbia ruled that E.P.A. had illegally loosened air pollution rules to help industries expand in areas that don't yet meet federal clean air standards. In all of these, courts found that the Administration had neither law nor scientific evidence to back its action.

Reagan's efforts to dismantle regulation legislatively have also failed miserably, and there is no reason to think he'll do any better in the more liberal 98th Congress. Early in Reagan's term, the Office of Management and Budget tried to persuade Congress to move the only agency with the word "consumer" in it, the Consumer Product Safety Commission, into the Commerce Department, the government's business advocacy agency. In the end, the proposal failed. Nor could O.M.B. coax the Senate to end the antitrust authority of the F.T.C., a move strongly opposed by Republican Senators John Danforth of Missouri and Slade Gorton of Washington. The two biggest legislative defeats for Reagan's deregulators were the Clean Air Act revisions and the "Regulatory Reform Bill." After much puffing, the Administration never even introduced its own Clean Air bill, settling instead for a mushy list of "principles" in mid-1981 that soon became legislatively irrelevant. The bill, which basically attempted to codify Reagan's cost-benefit principles and apply them to the independent regulatory agencies, passed the Senate 95 to 0, but stalled in the House dur-

ing the lame-duck session, when many committee chairmen, led
by John Dingell, objected to it in a Rules Committee session.

Conservatives bravely talk about cooking up a new batch of
deregulation measures in the 98th Congress. They intend to rein-
troduce legislation on clean air and regulatory reform, to weaken
the standard on carcinogens in food, and to allow OSHA to do
cost-benefit analyses. But the problems that thwarted them in the
97th Congress persist. The biggest Congressional problem is hostility toward appointees such as Anne Burford and James Watt,
whom one legislator has called "the Bonnie and Clyde of the
environment." George Eads of Rand concurs. He says that the Reaganites have "destroyed for a decade the ability to think about reform in a nonpartisan way. You can't talk intelligently about
changing the Clean Air Act because the first question is how Anne
[Burford] will enforce it. And that's the end of the discussion."
The dioxin disaster at Times Beach, Missouri, and the obvious
popularity of environmental issues in polls, i.e., the so-called
"green" vote, have exacerbated the Congressional reaction. This
confluence has noticeably shifted the axis of regulatory debate in
Congress. One now hears more of "toxic time bombs" than of
"overregulation."

At the same time, the deregulators to some extent have been
abandoned by their own political leaders. President Reagan, for
all his talk, has expended nowhere near as much of his personal
political capital on behalf of deregulatory measures as on his tax
and budget programs. As Christopher Demuth of O.M.B. somewhat defensively explained it, "No President spends much time
on regulatory matters." (Of course, no other President blamed
regulation for our economic decline and fall, either.) The President's lack of wholehearted support cut the steam behind the regulatory reform bill, and annoyed James Carty, head of regulatory
affairs at the National Association of Manufacturers. "We've been
working on this thing for four years," he complained in his office
recently. "We had the thing greased to go in 1981. If they had
jumped on it early, it would be law today. Instead, the White
House had lower echelon people working on it. Legislatively,
they've flunked."

All the Administration's deregulatory problems—
incompetence, Congressional revolt, legal constraints—have surfaced in its implementation of President Reagan's executive order
that requires executive agencies to prepare cost-benefit analyses
for all "major" regulations unless it is specifically precluded by
statute. It demands that benefits exceed costs before a regulation
can be promulgated, and puts O.M.B. in charge of compliance
with the order. Lengthy studies by the Library of Congress, the
House Energy and Commerce Committee, and the Alliance for
Justice concluded that O.M.B. implementation of the executive
order is probably an unlawful usurpation of agency regulatory authority. They also assert that O.M.B.'s review authority permits
unhappy businesses to seek political help in the White House, of
which O.M.B. is a part. As Representative Al Gore of Tennessee
asserted in a Congressional hearing:

I think it was no accident that only 30 days after a secret meeting between
O.M.B. and the Chemical Manufacturers Association, the hazardous
waste disposal regulations were ordered by O.M.B. to be reviewed . . .
that shortly after a secret meeting between the Air Transport Association
and the O.M.B., air carrier certification rules were designated for review
by O.M.B. . . . that shortly after a secret meeting between O.M.B. and
the American Mining Congress, the Interior Department's rule on ex-
traction of coal was postponed indefinitely.

In a speech to the U.S. Chamber of Commerce, C. Boyden
Gray, the counsel for George Bush's Task Force on Regulatory
Relief, went so far as to invite political intervention:

If you go to the agency first, don't be too pessimistic if they can't solve
the problem there. If they don't, that's what the task force is for. Two
weeks ago [a group] showed up and I asked if they had a problem. They
said they did, and we made a couple of phone calls and straightened it
out, alerted the top people at the agency that there was a little hanky-
panky going on at the bottom of the agency, and it was cleared up very
rapidly—so the system does work if you use it as a sort of an appeal. You
can act as a double check on the agency that you might encounter problems with.

This approach undermines the theory of administrative deci-
sionmaking by encouraging a secret political review of what
should be an on-the-record decision. As Washington lawyer Joan
Z. Bernstein put it, "It has been nonfacetiously suggested that the

lawyer who does not argue all the way to Vice President Bush may be subjecting himself to a malpractice charge. . . . I, for one, have already put the Vice President's number on my rolodex."

As for the executive order's cost-benefit test, agencies in the Reagan Administration actually appear more likely to apply a "cost-cost" test. Critics such as Representative Henry Waxman of California persuasively charge that because businesses control cost data, because benefit data (lives saved, injuries prevented, etc.) barely exist, because the long-range effects of many pollutants can't currently be measured, and because no formula can quantify value judgments like equity, strict cost-benefit tests are, in the words of a 1981 House Government Operations Committee report, "simply too primitive a tool to make a decisive factor in rule-making." The O.M.B. form entitled "Regulatory Docket Worksheet," which requires agencies to summarize information about a proposed regulation, has lines for entering all sorts of costs—"Federal Cost Impact," "Compliance Cost Impact," "Affected Public," "Consultations"—but there is no space at all for "Potential Benefits." And in an interview, O.M.B.'s Chris DeMuth acknowledged that "you can't really quantify benefits." But if you won't or can't estimate benefits, all the Administration's talk about cost-benefit analysis can't be anything but a hoax.

George Bush's task force claims that no less than $70 billion will be saved over a decade due to its deregulation program. But this number is based largely on data supplied by regulated businesses themselves. And it assumes that repealed regulations had *zero* benefit—that, for example, passive restraints would save no lives, even though experts concur that they would avoid 90,000 deaths and 600,000 serious injuries over a decade. Other agencies disagree. In the summer of 1981, O.M.B. estimated Administration deregulatory savings at $15 billion to $18 billion, but a year later, the number had fallen to $9 billion to $11 billion. Under Congressional questioning, F.T.C. chairman Jim Miller admitted that it was "conceivable" that later benefit studies could shrink the $9 billion to $11 billion to zero or negative, meaning that benefits would *exceed* costs.

Two years after launching its assault on the regulatory state, the Administration has run out of gas and credibility. And the

Reaganites seem to know it. "It's slower than I thought it would be," C. Boyden Gray told *Newsday.* "I think we made a mistake earlier about creating expectations. The rhetoric always gets ahead of you. . . . There isn't much power in the White House— not as much as the public thinks." At a recent business conference, Gray blamed the Administration's lack of success on powerful environmentalists and a press that "slants the issues." In one sense, Gray is right. Were it not for citizen groups litigating, the press exposing, and members of Congress probing, Reagan's deregulators might have succeeded in scuttling health and safety law enforcement. But when such critics threw the spotlight of scrutiny on the Administration, it blinked and faltered.

After all the foxy appointees, mismanagement, lost court cases, administrative about-faces, and legislative rejections—not to mention the incompetence, conflicts, and sweetheart settlements at E.P.A.—the Administration did it to itself. As F.T.C. commissioner Michael Pertschuk says, they're "the gang that couldn't deregulate straight."

BUDGETING STATES' RIGHTS[4]

It has been said that there are no new debates in politics, just old battles waged again on different turf with different rhetoric. A look ahead to deliberations on a federal budget which questions our very concept of public responsibility, and on a "New Federalism" which is at least two decades old, seems to confirm this adage.

All of our problems cannot be laid at President Reagan's door. Former presidents of both parties share in the responsibility for current conditions, as do the governors of the Federal Reserve Board. There are no quick and easy answers to our current dilemma, but some sound reasoning is needed in order to elicit a prudent

[4] Magazine article by Sar A. Levitan, research professor of economics and director of the Center for Social Policy Studies at The George Washington University. Published by Permission of Transaction, Inc. from *Society,* Vol. 14, #5. Copyright © 1982 by Transaction, Inc.

response. Given the long background to our present economic conditions, we cannot expect Reagan to fix overnight the mess he has helped create in the past year and a half.

The administration's ideological commitment to supply-side economics and to small and decentralized government is well known. For some, these concepts have assumed the stature of religious tenets, while for others they remain a category of voodoo superstitions. The administration has built its budget and its New Federalism proposal on three basic premises:

• Taxes have reached so prohibitive a level as to discourage investment and economic growth, making reductions in the federal tax burden the key to future economic expansion and budget stability.
• The private sector can more efficiently and effectively meet the needs of all but the "truly needy," and can respond adequately by providing employment, training, and diverse human services.
• Most federal social programs have failed, and those that address legitimate needs could be more effectively financed and administered at state and local levels.

The argument about whether these initiatives offer solutions to our present economic and social problems may not be soluble, but the foundations in which these assumptions are grounded should be examined.

Supply-Side Results

In 1981, President Reagan was successful in securing approval of his sweeping reductions in federal tax rates. Since that time, we have been awaiting the promised supply-side results, the great surge of investment and growth which was to be triggered by lower marginal tax rates. Those results have yet to appear. The end to the current recession is not yet in sight, interest rates have turned upward once again, and unemployment has reached disturbing levels.

The administration rejects any judgments of its programs at this time, claiming that it is too early to render a verdict. But here it is useful to return to the basic assumption. The Reagan tax program is built on a "theory of rational expectations," on the premise that investment will surge in anticipation of a more favorable economic climate fostered by government. There is nothing to wait for—either the tax and budget cuts generate optimism and expansion, or else it is "business as usual," with a smaller revenue pie as the result of tax reductions. As the deficit projections now show, we are getting the latter.

The assumption that marginal tax rates were prohibitively high has always been suspect among economists. Many Western European nations manage to maintain healthy rates of economic growth in spite of relative tax burdens heavier than ours. The course which the administration has chosen is looking increasingly like the traditional medicine—we are now battling inflation with tight monetary policy and high interests rates, beating prices down by creating idle capacity in our industries and placing millions of Americans on unemployment lines. It is not a novel response to inflation, but one we had previously seemed to reject.

The irony of the current situation is that by pursuing the speculative supply-side theory the administration has created a serious deficit problem, long the focal point of Republican criticism. We face the prospect later this year of a head-on collision between high deficits and a tight money policy, which will push interest rates even higher and choke off the beginnings of an economic recovery. The deficit problem is nearly unmanageable because we have written off too much of the federal tax base and because we have yet to adopt a realistic posture toward our current defense needs. The havoc created by supply-side economics cannot be corrected by adjustments in domestic spending—the potential "savings" sadly are not there.

If we are to return to a prudent course in charting our economic policy, we must begin with some realistic budget projections. In its attempts to disguise the magnitude of impending deficits, the administration has once again donned rose-colored glasses—pinning its hopes on such unlikely occurrences in 1983 as a growth rate for real GNP in excess of 5 percent, an inflation rate only slightly above 6 percent, and an interest rate on Treasury bills of only 10.5 percent. However, the Congressional Budget Office projected that, even assuming all of the president's proposed policy changes and budget cuts, the deficit for fiscal 1983 will reach $180 billion rather than the $91 billion claimed by the administration.

Surely the public interest is not well served by such wishful thinking, and such predictions only emphasize how strained the basic
supply-side assumptions about tax burdens have become.

Clearly, something must be done to control the rising cost of
entitlements. For example, while social security has been essential
to give our aged population a basic income, it is difficult to justify
a complete guarantee of the recipients' standard of living through
indexing at a time when the incomes of working people are suffering significant erosion. Similarly, there is little justification for
giving tax-exempt income to relatively affluent retired persons,
and the taxing of social security benefits in the same manner that
we tax unemployment insurance benefits should be a high priority. We have also failed to respond to soaring medical costs, which
have grossly inflated expenditures under health-care entitlement
programs. Yet rather than making realistic reforms to rein in these
entitlement programs, the administration has placed the burden
of budget "savings" on those who can least afford to bear it.

Relying on the Private Sector

These realizations bring us back to the administration's second
basic assumption, that the private sector can more effectively meet
the demands of most Americans. When one examines exactly
where most cuts in domestic spending are being made and considers who is bearing the burden of the shift back to the private sector,
it is difficult not to question the administration's intent.

Intentionally or otherwise, the tax and spending cuts enacted
last year are having an increasingly visible redistributive effect,
with net gains accruing to the wealthiest Americans while net losses are suffered by those in the lowest income groups. A well-
known economic consulting firm, A. Gary Shilling and Company,
has estimated that in fiscal year 1982 the top 5 percent of income
recipients will gain more than $9 billion in the aggregate as a re-
sult of the tax and budget cuts, while the roughly 30 percent of
all families at the lower end of the income spectrum stand to be
major losers. The supply-side ideology suggests that income gains
will eventually trickle down to the less fortunate. In the end, all
income groups will gain, and no one will lose, or so they say. In

the meantime, the "haves" of our nation will do quite well. In effect, the segment of society that is least able to afford it is being told: Pay now and you may fly later, if any seats remain.

Even if we take the administration at its word, if we accept the claim that the intent is not to redistribute income but to allow the private sector to fulfill more effectively the needs of Americans, its assumption about the private sector is far from convincing. Somehow we are asked to ignore the entire history of the New Deal and the Great Society, to refrain from asking why the federal government became involved in employment, training, education, human services, or income maintenance. The private sector is capable of many marvelous things, but it has inevitably fallen short of making adequate investments in human capital or providing some guarantee of adequate income. It was in response to this reality that we have sought—under both Democratic and Republican leadership—to improve the economic and social structure of this nation. Could we have possibly come so far over the past five decades without public commitments to education, to research and development, to jobs, and to an improved quality of life in our nation's cities?

It is perhaps most disturbing that many of the details of the administration's 1983 budget seem directly to contradict its rhetoric concerning self-sufficiency and the private sector. A study released in February by the Center for the Study of Social Policy found that the working poor in 24 states will be better off quitting their jobs and relying entirely on welfare if proposed cuts and rule changes in the AFDC (Aid to Families with Dependent Children) program are adopted. The 1983 budget suggests reductions in AFDC costs both through less liberal treatment of outside earnings and through presumed savings attributed to work requirements, even though the former gives recipients less reason to work and the latter offers unrealistic promises of private-sector jobs for the unskilled amidst 9 percent unemployment, and rising. If the administration were serious about putting employable AFDC recipients to work, the generation or location of useful jobs would require more federal funds rather than less—the administration ought to have learned that there is no free lunch.

There is no explanation for how the private sector will provide the education, training, and employment now supported with public funds, particularly given current economic conditions. The 1983 budget would slash federal aid for education by $2.7 billion, including reductions in compensatory and special education as well as the elimination of some 700,000 college grants. Private philanthropy offers no substitute. Ignoring both the current high unemployment and the rise in displaced workers whose skills are becoming obsolete, the budget would further cut funds for employment and training. In an approach reminiscent of the "let-them-eat-cake" philosophy, unemployed workers who do manage to find and enroll in training programs will be denied stipends. Perhaps the new slogan will be "let-them-eat-training." In any case, even if the overall job picture improves in 1983, there is no reason to believe that the private sector has adequate incentives to invest in the unskilled and deficiently educated workers who need a helping hand to be self-sufficient.

Finally, there presumably is one caveat to the administration's reliance on the private sector—an admission that the federal government retains a responsibility to assist the "truly needy." We can argue about the definition of need, and in fact the administration has continually redefined its concept of the truly needy to serve its changing budget constraints. Yet the administration is now abandoning even its own standards; under the 1983 budget proposals, the average combined monthly AFDC, food-stamp, and fuel-aid benefit for a mother with two small children who has no job and no other income would fall nationally from $450 to $423, according to a recent study. Energy-assistance payments would be treated totally as income in AFDC, even though this fuel aid is directly tied to an essential need of poor households. Food-stamp benefits would be similarly adjusted, and work incentives in the program would be weakened. Then, having exhausted all rationales, food-stamp and child-nutrition funds are arbitrarily slashed further, and the summer meal program for poor children entirely abandoned. The reason given by the Office of Management and Budget for eliminating the summer meal program is that it has been "riddled with fraud and abuse." That is one way of punishing criminals—by denying poor children meals in the summer. God help the kids who turn to the private sector for their food next summer.

Past Failures and New Federalism

Having looked briefly at the administration's supply-side ideology and belief in the private sector, we now come to the third major assumption underlying current policies, the idea that federal social programs have been a failure and that those serving legitimate goals could be better developed at state and local levels. This assumption embodies two very separate and distinct ideas, both of which must be accepted if one is to embrace the New Federalism. Upon close examination, the case is not convincing.

The claim that federal social programs have failed is simply contrary to fact. Certainly, if one measures the success of the Great Society programs by their impact on poverty in America, their achievements are impressive. When President Johnson first launched his Great Society program, thirty-six million Americans were counted as poor. A dozen years later, the official number had been reduced by one-third, and the hardship of many more had been reduced through in-kind assistance in the form of food stamps, subsidized housing, and medical aid. Only within the last few years has the poverty rate started to rise once again, the combined result of loose labor markets and the failure of AFDC and other income-maintenance programs to keep pace with the rising cost of living. But for the twelve million Americans lifted from poverty, federal social programs surely have not failed.

The Great Society went further, of course, than basic income-maintenance programs. Equal employment opportunity laws opened up job opportunities for women and minorities that had been closed in the absence of government intervention. Millions of our youth have obtained a college education that would have otherwise been beyond their families' reach. Much of the insecurity that faced the aged and the needy even two decades ago has been eliminated. Collectively, it is a record of achievement of which we should be proud.

As in all bold undertakings, we have made our mistakes, which serve as lessons for the future. And in many ways, the bad name some of the programs have been given stems from expectations that were too high, from a belief that we could quickly change the nature of man and his institutions as a response to social problems. We have probably learned to expect a little less. We have no reason to label as failures those efforts which have wrought a host of important benefits.

As for the greater effectiveness of state and local governments in taking on such programs and challenges, it seems that we need to make a distinction between decentralized administration and decentralized responsibility. One of the lessons we have learned in the past two decades, for example in the CETA program, is that a decentralized system of administration can be both appropriate and highly effective in bringing federal resources to bear on diverse state and local problems. Yet in many areas, our history tells us that federal responsibility and financing are essential—state and local governments lack both the resources to support such endeavors and the jurisdictional scope to address problems that are truly national in nature. Welfare benefits should be accepted as a federal responsibility from the perspectives of both equity and efficacy, and the principle applies to a number of government efforts to ensure income adequacy and equal opportunity.

It is appropriate to think about roles and functions in a federal system, but the administration's swap of Medicaid for AFDC and food stamps offers no coherent rationale that would strengthen or clarify relationships between federal, state, and local levels. So we are left again questioning this New Federalism's ultimate intent. The administration is urging a sweeping revision of the way in which we finance and administer domestic programs on the simple article of faith that government close to the people is more responsive and more effective. Yet we also know that the rights of minorities—economic, racial, cultural, or whatever—have usually been protected and preserved only through federal action. In the absence of a compelling rationale that clarifies federal, state, and local functions, it is hard not to wonder whether the administration is really looking for a back door through which to discard a range of existing social programs. Too many statehouses have displayed no eagerness to take over the programs which the administration would bequeath to them.

The public has heard much already about the specifics of the New Federalism, including its questionable financing mechanisms. To make up for the transfer of responsibility to states, the federal government will make available to them funds from excise taxes, more than half of which will be accounted for from the windfall profits tax on oil. This transfer of funds will last only for the initial four years, after which time the states will be free either to impose their own taxes or give up on these programs. But since more than half of the transfer comes from the windfall profits tax on oil that would not be available to most states, they would have to resort to new taxes to cover program costs.

Another problem is that the exise taxes are not necessarily related to inflation. Most of them are imposed in terms of unit costs (i.e., so many cents per gallon of gasoline or so many cents per pack of cigarettes). It would therefore be difficult for the states to maintain the current revenues from the excise taxes. State and local governments already vary widely in their reliance on excise taxes as a revenue source, and the implicit promise that there will be no new losers in the transfer of programs to states seems virtually impossible to keep.

One Nation

State and local governments must be strong partners with the federal government. Citizens do not walk into a federal AFDC office, a federal office for unemployment insurance, or a federal social service office. They walk into state and local offices, and the officials who administer those programs must have the ability to respond effectively to the problems which they face.

We live in one nation. In an era when so many of our economic and social problems take on global proportions, a return to an outmoded concept of states' rights may not be in our collective best interests. The real meaning of federalism is a form of government where powers are shared among all levels of government, not one in which the federal government abdicates its responsibility to address social problems.

WHAT REALLY HAPPENED AT EPA[5]

During a 1980 campaign stop in Salt Lake City, Ronald Reagan made a fateful commitment to a group of Western ranchers. "I am one who supports the Sagebrush Rebellion," he declared. "Count me in as a rebel."

In a bizarre sequence of events, that commitment allied President Reagan with an extremist group of anti-environmentalists, led directly to his troubles with the Environmental Protection Agency—and may have put him irretrievably on the losing side of a much larger war. To understand these ramifications, begin at the beginning. The Sagebrush Rebellion was led by Western cattle and sheep men who graze their herds on a Texas-size domain of arid, government-owned rangeland run by the Interior Department's Bureau of Land Management. Over the years the pounding of too many hoofs and the nibbling of too many mouths have turned many BLM pastures into dust bowls during dry months and seas of mud when it rains. The pollution of Western rivers and air by the half-billion tons of topsoil that blows and flows off the public lands each year is one of the country's most serious environmental problems.

Until about ten years ago the stockmen succeeded in resisting most BLM attempts to reduce herd size. But in the 1970s conservation groups won a series of court orders and Congressional battles designed to force BLM to crack down on overgrazing. The Sagebrush Rebellion was the ranchers' response: a counterattack to break BLM once and for all by getting Congress to turn its vast domain over to the states.

Trusty Troika

When Ronald Reagan became President, he fulfilled his commitment to the rebels in a startling way: he brought them to Washington and allowed them to set up a command post inside

[5] Magazine article by James Nathan Miller, editor. *Reader's Digest.* 123:59–64. Jl. '83. Reprinted with permission from the July 1983 Reader's Digest. Copyright © 1983 by The Reader's Digest Assn., Inc.

the Interior Department from which they issued recommendations on environmental appointments.

Calling the shots behind these recommendations was Joseph Coors, a Colorado millionaire and member of Reagan's "Kitchen Cabinet"—close political allies who had a strong voice in top-level appointments. Coors (whose money comes from the Coors beer company and from interests in energy development) is widely considered one of the country's leading anti-environmentalists. In 1977, to give legal teeth to his views, he led a group of wealthy ranchers, oil men and mining executives in founding the Mountain States Legal Foundation. MSLF specialized in suits against Interior and EPA that hampered enforcement of clean-air-and-water and wilderness-protection laws, thus supporting the goals of the Sagebrush Rebellion.

So many Coors followers got jobs in the Administration that they became known as Reagan's "Colorado Mafia." For the top three members, those jobs just happened to involve the environment. The first was James Watt, president of MSLF. He was named Interior Secretary. The second was Robert Burford, a wealthy Colorado rancher and mining engineer (with grazing rights on 32,000 BLM acres) who had been a leader of the Sagebrush Rebellion's fight to destroy BLM. He was appointed director of BLM.

The third appointment was Anne Gorsuch, a real-estate and labor lawyer for the Mountain Bell Telephone Co. Gorsuch was a member of the Colorado legislature, where she had been part of a Republican faction known for its unconventional legislative tactics and extreme anti-government-regulation views. Gorsuch and Burford were close personally (they later married), and she had the endorsement of Coors and Watt. The President made her head of EPA.

The choice of EPA's chief is critical, in terms both of the national interest and of the President's credibility. EPA is the keystone of the entire structure of environmental-protection laws enacted in the 1960s and '70s. Just to name these laws—which burdened the economy with billions of dollars of extra costs while producing benefits that were slow in coming and often invisible—is to recall also the intensity of opposition to them by industry and

agriculture: Clean Air Act, Surface Mining Control and Recla-
mation Act, Wilderness Act, Toxic Substances Control Act, and
on and on.

EPA writes and enforces the complex technical specifications
the new laws demand. Its scientific competence is crucial to the
nation's physical well-being; its administrative credibility is crucial to the nation's *sense* of well-being. Moreover, every recent national poll on the question has shown that the need to preserve the
environment—even at substantial economic sacrifice—is the one
major domestic issue on which Democrats and Republicans overwhelmingly agree.

Silent Revolution

But EPA is above all a *regulatory* agency, and therein lies a
problem. One of Ronald Reagan's strongest convictions is that unnecessary government regulations are the chief cause of many of
the most serious problems of American industry. When Watt,
Burford and Gorsuch arrived in Washington, they knew precisely
what the President wanted them to do: deregulate the environment. They developed two main tactics:

The first was to staff top levels of their agencies with industry
lawyers, lobbyists, press agents—people whose chief experience
lay in fighting the very regulations they were now expected to enforce.

No important environmental post went to a person recommended by environmentalists. To head what is perhaps EPA's
most critical operation, its toxic-waste cleanup program, Gorsuch
selected Rita Lavelle, a public-relations woman with Aerojet-
General, a California company with one of the state's worst wa-
ter-pollution problems. The chief EPA regulatory-reform post
was given to a former consultant to Dow Chemical Co. As its pes-
ticide expert EPA recruited a consultant for an industry-
supported research group. The post of general counsel went to an
Exxon lawyer, the clean air spot to a lobbyist for the American
Paper Institute.

The story was the same in Watt's Interior Department. To
advise him on administration of the Alaska Lands Act, Watt

named the lobbyist who had fought the act's passage on behalf of Alaskan industry. To head the Office of Surface Mining, he appointed an Indiana state legislator who had sponsored a resolution challenging the constitutionality of certain provisions of the federal strip-mining law.

Perhaps the most remarkable appointment was the new Assistant Secretary of Agriculture. This position, which involves control of the Forest Service, went to John Crowell, general counsel of Louisiana-Pacific Corp., one of the largest timber cutters in the national forests. At the time of Crowell's appointment, a subsidiary of his company was being sued in a civil case for violating federal anti-trust laws; in order to freeze a small competitor out of operations in Alaska's Tongass National Forest, the subsidiary had conspired to reduce the price of Forest Service timber. It later lost the case.

These appointments added up to a silent revolution. In a few months they put the environmental structure so painstakingly developed over two decades into the hands of the very people who had led the fight against its creation. When Congress finally looked into the way Gorsuch and her appointees were running EPA, it quickly became clear that they were running it just as if they were still working for their former employers. Consider:

Gorsuch told excutives of a New Mexico refinery that they did not have to abide by EPA's lead-in-gasoline standards since she did not intend to enforce them while they were being reviewed.

EPA officials testified that John Hernandez, Gorsuch's second-in-command, allowed Dow Chemical to censor out of an EPA report the finding that the company had grossly polluted its headquarters town of Midland, Mich., with the toxic chemical dioxin. (When this revelation cost Hernandez his job, the Energy Department immediately gave him a temporary appointment as a $245-a-day consultant.)

James Sanderson, Gorsuch's choice for third-in-command and a former lawyer for Coors, did legal work on environmental matters for Coors and others from his EPA desk.

Louis Cordia, a former specialist on EPA at a Coors-supported think tank, was given the job of compiling a "hit list" of EPA officials who were too tough on industry. In the Denver office, for instance, 13 lawyers suspected of being anti-business were reclassified as junior toxic-waste inspectors. (They were later reinstated.) The office's water-quality director, a highly respected scientist, was ordered to transfer to an unspecified new job in Washington; when he refused to accept without being told what the job was, he was fired.

The Administration's second deregulation technique was revealed in an incautious remark Watt made shortly after taking office. "We will use the budget system," he told a convention of national park concessionaires, "to be the excuse to make major policy decisions." Here are two examples of how this worked:

Burford used budget cuts to reduce the staff of BLM's Range Management Division from 1040 full-time employees in 1982 to a planned 795 in 1984, with further cuts expected. So effective has Burford been in crippling the division's efforts to prevent overgrazing that Watt has already proclaimed victory for the Sagebrush Rebels in their battle against BLM. Today, he says, he's "a rebel without a cause."

In her first two budgets, Gorsuch cut EPA's funds by 30 percent. She was able to do this while EPA's responsibilities were growing rapidly, she said, mainly because she was turning many of its functions over to the states. But during the same period she reduced EPA's contributions to the states by 20 percent.

Last November, when a House subcommittee asked Gorsuch for documents to show how Lavelle had run the toxic-waste cleanup program, President Reagan ordered Gorsuch to refuse to provide them. He said the documents were "enforcement sensitive"—i.e., they would tip off industry to EPA legal tactics in cracking down on polluters.

This refusal led, first, to a contempt-of-Congress citation of Gorsuch (the only such citation of a Cabinet official in history) and then to a decision by a federal judge urging the Administration to compromise its differences with Congress. When the documents finally became public, it turned out that their main enforcement-sensitive information was the revelation of how little enforcement there had been.

Reagan's critics have cited a couple of hundred examples of what his anti-environmental policies have done to key units of the environmental structure. For instance:

Council on Environmental Quality. In 1970 Congress created the CEQ to give the President scientific guidance. Reagan reduced its budget from $2.5 million to $926,000 and replaced the professional staff with inexperienced political appointees. Last March CEQ chairman Alan Hill admitted that in two years in office he had never discussed environmental matters with Reagan.

Office of Air Quality. OAQ has reversed its pre-Reagan call for urgent action on acid rain, now claiming the need for years of further research. It has also recommended reductions in auto-exhaust standards that would allow Detroit to double the carbon-monoxide and nitrogen-oxide pollution emitted by its cars.

National Park Service. Watt has slashed the land-acquisition budget for parks from a pre-Reagan annual average of $210 million to a planned $55 million for 1984.

Office of Surface Mining. Watt's OSM has reduced its strip-mine inspection staff from 145 (which environmentalists said was far too few to do the job) to 69.

Forest Service. Under lumberman Crowell, USFS has asked Congress for an additional $50 million (an 11-percent rise) for building subsidized roads for logging companies, while requesting $1.6 million less (a 16-percent drop) for maintaining hiking trails. (The agency has also been stonewalling Congress in the anti-trust case involving Crowell's former employer. Claiming its documents are enforcement-sensitive, it has refused to give them to Congress—or even to say how much money the government lost in the case.)

Today there is a widespread feeling that the Reagan Administration is deliberately trying to destroy the environmental structure. Last year Russell Train, a conservative Republican who headed EPA under Presidents Nixon and Ford, had this to say about Gorsuch's firings of enforcement officials: "It is hard to imagine any manager undertaking such a personnel policy unless its purpose was to destroy the enterprise." Dan Lufkin, a conservative Republican who headed Reagan's pre-Presidential advisory task force on environmental matters, wrote to the President: "The Administration's plan is to create an unworkable, unenforceable, impractical and ineffective travesty of regulation."

End of the Battle?

Will the environmental structure be destroyed under this Administration? The answer is clearly no. It is badly damaged, and will require time to repair. But it is inconceivable that the public will allow a fringe group of extremists to destroy it. The backlash against today's environmental policies has been ferocious, in Congress and around the country. Both the Democratic House and Republican Senate have voted overwhelmingly against Administration proposals to weaken environmental laws. Present signs are that Congress's ultimate reaction will be to toughen the laws.

What hope is there that Reagan will change his environmental policies? At the moment, none. "This Administration," says the President, "can be proud of its record in environmental protection." Even when he was forced to accept Gorsuch's resignation, he did it with a letter saying: "Anne, you can walk out of EPA with your head held high. You have served this nation well." And he says he won't ask her successor at EPA (William Ruckelshaus, who served under President Nixon as the agency's first head) to change basic policies. "I'm too old to change," Reagan told reporters.

The environmentalists are just as adamant. They say they won't be satisfied with anything *less* than basic policy changes—not only at EPA but at BLM, the Office of Surface Mining, the Forest Service and all the rest.

So the battle will almost certainly spread. Congressional investigators are shifting their attention from the conflicts of interest under Gorsuch to what appear to be equally serious cases of pro-industry bias under Watt, Burford and Crowell. Inevitably, as they dig into these cases, the issue will focus less and less on how much damage Watt and the others can do to the environmental structure, and more and more on how much damage Ronald Reagan's environmental policies can do to Ronald Reagan.

EDITOR'S INTRODUCTION

There is great controversy over just how much Reaganomics has hurt the poor. Cuts in Federal programs have trimmed aid to those working people who are just over the officially defined poverty level. The budget cuts hit especially hard at food stamps, school lunches and aid to families with dependent children.

The Reagan administration argues that its successful fight against inflation helps the poor and the near-poor more than social programs that tended to encourage people to remain on public assistance. By lowering inflation from double-digit annual rates to near 4 percent, Reagan can claim that "people at the poverty level have about $600 more in [annual] purchasing power . . . than they would have if inflation had stayed at the [previous] level." The official poverty level is $9,287 for a family of four.

A report in *Fortune Magazine* makes the point that just as it is impossible to determine who benefits and how much from social programs, so it is impossible to tell who has been hurt the most by the cutbacks. The article concludes that the old, expensive social programs have done nothing to decrease poverty. Thomas Eagleton, Democratic Senator from Missouri, presents the opposing case in the *Atlantic*. He points to the achievements of legislation that has done much to alleviate the suffering of the poor, and takes the position that "a decent society" takes responsibility for the "pressing problems" that afflict a relatively small portion of its population. Nick Kotz, in an article from *The New Republic,* provides evidence of the harsh consequences of Reagan's effort to dismantle federal social welfare.

The next two articles in this section deal with the theory that urban poverty and center city deterioration can best be dealt with by involving the private sector rather than relying on government aid. In *The New Republic,* James Traub, a freelance writer, is not hopeful that private enterprise will accomplish a great deal in urban centers. He points out that these run-down areas need improved local, municipal services before they can hope to attract businesses. But reductions in Federal aid now make the creation of such vital services impossible.

In the *Harvard Business Review,* George Cabot Lodge, professor of business administration at the Harvard Business School, and William R. Glass, associates fellow, approach the problem of the center city from the point of view of business. They outline the difficulties companies face when they try to work with the community to improve neighborhoods and train the unemployed.

HAS REAGAN HURT THE POOR?[1]

The dispute has been waged mainly with politicized rhetoric and arguable projections about the future. Reagan justifies reversing nearly 50 years of increasing federal efforts to redistribute income on the ground that the resulting programs don't really help the poor and now cost more than the nation can afford. The Administration contends that it wants to replace fiscal profligacy with sanity and to reduce federal largess to the middle class, business, and special-interest groups long favored by Democrats. Such a course, it argues, would free up enough money for the genuinely needy.

The big tax cuts enacted by Congress in 1981 are indisputably returning more dollars to high-income than low-income households. After all, taxes were reduced by the same 23 percent over three years for all income brackets. Counting budget cuts as well, some poor people evidently will be worse off than they were. Those most affected, however, are apt to be families just *above* the government's official poverty line.

The Administration contends that the material well-being of the poor and near-poor—at least those able to work—may depend more on the economy, especially the availability of jobs, than on

[1] Reprint of magazine article by Gurney Breckenfeld. *Fortune.* 107:77+. Ja. 24, '83. Reprinted by permission.

cuts in their taxes or transfer payments. "A robust economy is absolutely fundamental to real opportunity," says Michael Horowitz, special counsel to David Stockman, director of the Office of Management and Budget. "We will get nowhere without it." With that in mind, some political pundits contend that the "fairness issue" might be almost forgotten by now if the U.S. economy had rebounded as the Administration envisaged two years ago. Instead, as unemployment has risen to the highest level since 1940, so has the clamor about Reagan policies.

The economy has also hampered Reagan's efforts to wallop two elephantine targets. He took office vowing "to curb the size and influence of the federal establishment" and to make drastic changes in welfare policies. The federal tax burden did fall from 21.4 percent of gross national product in fiscal 1981 to 20.3 percent in the fiscal year ending last September 30—but at the cost of a record budget deficit. Social spending as a share of national output actually rose, partly because the recession lifted outlays for such programs as unemployment compensation. In his effort to leave the "truly needy" unhurt, Reagan has concentrated on persuading Congress to pare subsidies for people able to work. He has been successful in tightening eligibility rules and benefit formulas for welfare programs in ways that mainly affect working people just above poverty.

Congress bore down hard on food stamps, school lunches, and aid to families with dependent children, the main federal-state welfare program; a lot of this aid goes to people above the poverty line. Reagan successfully urged legislators to curtail financial incentives that encourage welfare mothers to work. At last count only 14.1 percent did work under the incentive program, vs. 14.9 percent before incentives were adopted in 1968. When incentives were cut back, sociologists predicted the mothers would quit and return to the full-time dole. So far, few have.

Unfortunately, efforts to measure vital details, notably how many people have been (or will be) hurt by how much and for how long, are thwarted by a warped statistical yardstick. The official government scorekeeper on income distribution, the Census Bureau, annually reports gross incomes before payroll and income taxes. The bureau counts government cash subsidies as income, but not subsidies in kind—such as medical care, food stamps, school lunches, and housing. Yet these non-cash subsidies now go to one U.S. household in six, and they account for two of every three federal dollars spent to aid the poor. Any measure that ignores them fails to reflect the real world.

Only two serious efforts have been made so far to calculate how deep Reagan cuts go and their impact on families and individuals. The Urban Institute, a nonprofit, Washington-based think tank, and the Congressional Budget Office have issued elaborate projections of how the 1981 tax and budget cuts will affect households across the entire spectrum of income brackets. The detail is not necessarily matched by accuracy, partly because the conceptual shortcomings in Census data can magnify the pain of the poor.

In a recent and critical book, *The Reagan Experiment,* the Urban Institute complains that there are too many "important unknowns" to permit a complete assessment of Reagan's changes. The study limited itself to cuts in taxes, food stamps, and aid to families with dependent children, omitting two dozen other subsidy programs for individuals. Nevertheless, the broad conclusions seem reasonable. The study determined that the changes "will provide modest income gains (after taxes and transfers) for the average household." Upper-income families will have "quite large" gains while "low-income families will experience a small net loss." The largest blow was found to fall on "working poor and near-poor families," particularly two million recipients of aid to families with dependent children who have incomes up to 75 percent above the poverty line.

The influential Congressional Budget Office issued a hasty and arguably slipshod forecast, which has figured prominently in the political wrangling about fairness. The CBO estimated that 85 percent of the cuts in individual federal income taxes will go to households with incomes above $20,000 a year in 1983, while two-thirds of the cuts in subsidies for individuals would fall on households with incomes below that level. For the same year, when the last phase of the tax cut takes effect, the CBO balanced the loss of cash and in-kind benefits against the gains from tax cuts. It reported that average households at opposite ends of the income spectrum would be affected as follows:

	LESS THAN $10,000	$80,00 AND OVER
Cash benefits lost	$ -270	$ -70
Tax cuts	120	15,250
Net	-150	15,180
In-kind benefits lost	-90	-50
Net including in-kind benefits	-240	15,130

The CBO analysis has been reported uncritically in the *New York Times, Newsweek,* the *National Journal,* and many other publications. But the presentation loads the dice in several ways. The statistical norm is to divide income groups into roughly equal fifths of the population. Yet only 1½ percent of households have incomes of $80,000 or more, so why didn't the CBO follow the norm? "If you use quintiles, the cutoff at the top is too low," explains CBO analyst Patricia Ruggles. "The tax changes had the greatest impact at high income, and we wanted to show that."

The CBO valued in-kind subsidies at their cost to the government, which exaggerates their worth to recipients, according to some studies, by as much as 65 percent. In addition, the study deducted the losses in in-kind benefits from incomes that did not include the value of in-kind benefits in the first place. The Office of Management and Budget objects to that kind of scorekeeping. OMB contends that excluding in-kind benefits from household incomes understates the income base and thus overstates the effect of the benefit cuts. Moreover, says OMB, the CBO failed to take into account the small average size and smaller income needs of households with incomes from $10,000 down. Some 49 percent of them were one-person households in 1981, compared with only 14 percent for other income groups. Before the 1981 tax cuts, fewer than half were poor if income is measured on the CBO basis. In sum, the conclusions about the lowest income group are wildly distorted.

Completed in a mere three weeks, the CBO study appears to have been tailored to provide political ammunition. It was requested by two Democrats, Ernest F. Hollings of South Carolina, ranking minority member of the Senate Budget Committee, and

Oklahoma's James R. Jones, chairman of the House Budget Committee. "There's no question that if it had been requested by Senator [Pete V.] Domenici [Republican chairman of the Senate Budget Committee] it would have been done differently," says Joseph Minarik, a CBO tax analyst. Minarik also reports that CBO's figures for in-kind benefits were based on "extremely thin" data—an observation that conveys a considerable probability of error.

In defending his economic program, President Reagan has proved equally adept at citing figures that critics fault as misleading. For instance, he has pointed to the unexpectedly swift decline of consumer price inflation, from 13.5 percent in 1980 to about 4.5 percent last year. Thanks to this, he observed at a September press conference, "people at the poverty level have about $600 more in [annual] purchasing power . . . and a median income family about $1,500 more than they would have had if inflation had stayed at the level it was when we started." That argument is only half right because it omits two facts: most subsidies are indexed to inflation, and incomes for the working poor tend to rise with prices.

By failing to count in-kind transfers as income, government figures years ago lost their usefulness for measuring changes in income distribution. With in-kind subsidies left out, the distribution of income has been remarkably constant. Families with the lowest fifth of incomes had 5 percent of the total in 1947, 1962, and 1981. For the same years, families in the highest fifth had 43.2 percent, 41.3 percent, and 41.9 percent. The figures weren't bad until the late Sixties, when in-kind subsidies grew large enough to make a big difference. The Census Bureau has not yet measured such aid accurately enough to publish incomes that include it, though the bureau hopes to do so by 1985.

Timothy Smeeding, associate professor of economics at the University of Utah and a consultant to the bureau, explains the difficulty: "It is impossible to determine with any acceptable degree of accuracy which persons benefited how much and from what programs." Distribution of in-kind subsidies is notoriously uneven. The latest Census count found that 29 percent of the official poor did not receive any, while 22 percent received at least three kinds. In another recent study for census, Smeeding used three methods to calculate the value of five big programs of non-cash subsidies. Depending on the method used, the transfers would have cut the number of poor in 1979 anywhere from 12 percent to 42 percent.

The official poverty level is also based on pretax incomes including cash but not in-kind subsidies. Having been adjusted annually for inflation, the threshold below which poverty officially begins is currently $9,287 for a family of four; however, it ranges from $4,620 for a one-person household to $18,572 for a family of nine or more. From 17.3 percent in 1965, official poverty dipped to a low of 11.1 percent in 1973, rose erratically to 11.4 percent in 1978, and since then has increased steadily to a 1981 level of 14 percent. But most economists and sociologists who have investigated the matter agree that the official rate grossly overstates the number of persons who actually ought to be considered poor.

If you include in-kind subsidies, U.S. poverty drops to about half the official level, with an important proviso. The value of the subsidies must be stated conservatively, at their calculated worth to recipients, not the (often much higher) cost to the government. Estimates by Smeeding and Sheldon Danziger at the University of Wisconsin's Institute for Research on Poverty put poverty after in-kind transfers at only 6.2 percent in 1972 and 6.1 percent in 1979. Danziger estimates that the figure moved up to 8 percent in 1981, partly because of rising unemployment.

If in-kind subsidies are valued at their full cost to the government, it is possible to argue that poverty in the U.S. virtually disappeared years ago. Counting the full cost to the government of food stamps, school lunches, several housing-subsidy programs, Medicare and Medicaid, G. William Hoagland, a congressional budget analyst, concluded that the incidence of poverty fell to 4.1 percent in 1980. Probably the most famous, and vigorously disputed, assertion of this genre came in 1978 from economist Martin Anderson, later a domestic policy adviser to President Reagan, who declared flatly: "The war on poverty has been won."

Most people doubt in these times of tent cities that the megabillions spent to help low-income groups have won the war. For one thing, three recessions interspersed with stagflation have sapped the economy's job-creating power. Even more important, major demographic changes have given poverty a depressing new configuration. The surge in divorce, separation, and illegitimate births in the Seventies helped to increase the number of one-parent families by 69 percent. Today more than one half of them are poor or near-poor and they constitute nearly a fifth of all families with children. Census Director Bruce Chapman calls the one-parent family the "newly significant factor" in both poverty and growing social spending. "Poverty levels for year-round, full-time workers have fallen close to zero," he notes, while for the few full-time workers who remain poor the reason is "primarily large family size, not low salaries,"

Family breakup has hit blacks especially hard. Separation, often a euphemism for abandonment, rose from 172 per 1,000 married persons in 1971 to 225 per 1,000 in 1981 (compared with a rise among white families from 21 to 29 per 1,000). Illegitimate births, up from 5.3 percent of all U.S. births in 1960 to 17 percent in 1979, leaped among blacks from 22 percent in 1960 to 55 percent in 1979. Increasingly the mothers are teenagers.

The contrast in prospects between those at the opposite ends of the economic spectrum is stark. At least 70 percent of today's poor, Smeeding says, are aged, disabled, or in households headed by a lone female parent with at least one preschool-age child. These people can't be expected to work much. Indeed, at last count the poor worked only about one-third as many hours a year as did the heads of households in the top income bracket.

When he launched the war on poverty in 1964, Lyndon Johnson said he wanted "to offer the forgotten fifth of our people opportunity and not doles." The evidence now is that help has been given, but we have made little progress in getting people off the dole and on their feet. The whole net gain against poverty, Smeeding and other authorities argue, can be attributed to transfer payments. Poverty measured with no subsidies at all stood at 21.3 percent in 1965 and 21.9 percent in 1980. Unless some politically acceptable way is found to improve on this grim record, the chances of true progress against poverty are bleak.

PROGRAMS WORTH SAVING[2]

A sense of the Democratic Party's retreat since Ronald Reagan's election is manifest in the tendency of Democrats to apoligize for the excesses of previous Democratic administrations. It is also apparent in what often seems a note of embarrassment when a Democrat speaks in defense of programs that involve the federal government, cost money, and help the needy—the poor, the uneducated, the malnourished, the handicapped, and the victims of discrimination.

A decent society tries to solve its pressing problems even when they directly afflict only a limited sector of the population. An effective government deals with pressing problems when circumstances permit the formation of the political coalition needed to support change. The period of unprecedented economic prosperity we experienced during the 1960s, featuring steady growth and negligible inflation, allowed the government to turn to problems that had been unaddressed for years. The result was an explosion of Great Society legislation; we took major steps against discrimination, poverty, hunger, lack of educational opportunity, and environmental degradation.

Obviously, today's changed political climate, produced in large part by economic hard times, has eroded support for some programs, particularly those narrowly targeted to the needs of the poor or minorities. This is a political reality that no one can deny. Moreover, if we are to succeed in controlling the federal budget, in order to bring down inflation and interest rates, these programs will be forced to compete for a piece of the shrinking federal pie, and to make do with less.

But recognizing these realities is one thing; it is quite another to say, as many do, that all of the programs were ill conceived from the outset; that we've devoted too much time, attention, and money to the needy and deprived; that the programs have failed; or that the need for the efforts no longer exists. Democrats have a compel-

[2] Magazine article by Thomas F. Eagleton, senator from Missouri. *Atlantic.* 250:8+ Jl.'82. Copyright © 1980, by The Atlantic Monthy Company, Boston, Mass. Reprinted with permission.

ling responsibility to stand against a conservative tide by affirming the value of these programs, which have succeeded and remain essential. Here are some examples.

The food stamp program has become so symbolic of a federal program gone bad that Senator Jesse Helms and his ultra-conservative Congressional Club recently used it as the centerpiece in a national fund-raising campaign. "Your contribution will be used by the Congressional Club to expose one of the most expensive, most abused and badly managed programs in the federal budget—food stamps," their letter stated. "Your contribution for as little as $15 can help save the American taxpayers *billions of dollars* in the years ahead."

Is there fraud in the program? Yes. Is the program abused? Undoubtedly. Should the program be terminated or gutted? Definitely not. According to the most recent survey data available, 78 percent of the 22 million food-stamp recipients are children, elderly, disabled persons, or single-parent heads of households. More than half of all food-stamp households have gross incomes of less than $3,600 per year, and an equal number have no liquid assets at all. Ninety-three percent of food-stamp recipients have liquid assets of less than $500.

Those who rant about food-stamp ripoffs forget the conditions that led to the creation of the food-stamp program in the 1960s. In 1967, a team of physicians, sponsored by the Field Foundation, traveled throughout the Mississippi Delta, the coal fields of Appalachia, and coastal South Carolina to study hunger among the people of America. What they found, in their own words, was shocking. "Wherever we went and wherever we looked, we saw children in significant numbers who were hungry and sick, children for whom hunger is a daily fact of life, and sickness, in many forms, an inevitability."

Ten years later, another team of physicians visited the same areas. Although many of the outward signs of poverty were still present, the extent of malnutrition, of hunger, was appreciably reduced. The reason for this dramatic change, in the opinion of both the doctors and the people they visited, was the food-stamp program.

Congress has taken significant action over the past few years to reduce the incidence of fraud and abuse in the program. Asset tests were tightened to ensure that people who owned luxury cars and vacation homes would not be eligible. Those disqualified from program participation for fraud are now required to repay the amount fraudulently obtained. States have been given incentives to reduce errors in issuing food stamps. Provisions regarding food stamps for aliens have been substantially revised, and virtually all college students are ineligible. By the end of 1980, before President Reagan took office, Congress had already enacted laws that eliminated nearly 1.5 million participants from the program and reduced the pool of persons potentially eligible for the program by more than 6 million.

The Omnibus Budget and Reconciliation Act of 1981 continued that trend. It terminated households with gross incomes that exceed 130 percent of the income level designated as the poverty line—nearly 900,000 persons. But this legislation went far beyond tightening eligibility. In 1981, for the first time, the bulk of the savings came from reductions made in benefits for families with incomes *below the poverty line.*

These cuts will not reduce fraud and waste. They will mean only that most of the people who receive food stamps will have less food. They mark a retreat from our commitment to provide nutritional assistance, through cuts not only in food stamps but also in school lunches; in the special supplemental-feeding program for women, infants, and children; in nutrition education in our schools. For most of our population, the major nutritional worry is being overweight. Various books on how to diet dominate our best-seller lists. Without belittling that concern in any way, we should be sensitive to the appalling irony of taking steps that could mean the recurrence of starvation in this generally prosperous nation.

The Legal Services Corporation has long been a favorite target of those on the far right, who have repeatedly characterized the corporation as wasteful and bloated, and have accused it of financing "social engineering" and immersing itself in "social activism."

With the election of Ronald Reagan, the assault on the Legal Services Corporation acquired new intensity. President Reagan formed a deep dislike for legal services attorneys while he was governor of California, when legal actions brought by the California Rural Legal Assistance (CRLA) caused him significant embarrassment. Combining this animosity with a general interest in budget cutting, President Reagan and David Stockman have asked Congress to abolish the corporation. They propose that the governor of each state should decide whether or not to fund any kind of legal-services program from proposed federal block grants that have been targeted for other services.

The Legal Services Corporation exists to further perhaps the noblest of this country's historical ideals: equal justice for all. It came into being, in 1974, only after other ways of improving access to legal counsel for the poor had been tried and proven insufficient.

These programs, voluntarily developed by the legal profession, proved neither numerous enough nor broad enough to meet the needs of the economically disadvantaged. In 1964, civil legal-aid offices serving the poor reached fewer than one percent of those in need.

In response to that deficiency, in 1965, the federal government initiated a modest ($600,000) experimental legal-services program in the Office of Economic Opportunity (OEO). By 1974, the majority of Congress, supported by the Nixon Administration, agreed that the federal legal-services program needed to be continued and insulated from political pressures jeopardizing the attorneys' ability to represent their clients' best interests. The Legal Services Corporation was created.

As for the charge that the Legal Services Corporation is a tool for "social engineering," in fact the overwhelming part of the legal-services lawyer's work is concentrated on basic issues of survival—food, shelter, health, and income. Legal-services lawyers represent the elderly in a nursing home where care is abusive, the mother who is left without money to feed her family when a benefit check does not arrive, the poor who are forced to live in unheated apartments because their landlord has not paid the utility bill. Some observers have marveled that legal-services attorneys can withstand the tedium of the average caseload.

Opponents of the corporation rail against misuse of class-action suits by legal-services attorneys. Some abuses have occurred, and Congress has prohibited legal-services attorneys from initiating lawsuits on certain subjects. For the most part, however, the class-action suits have been undertaken to protect poor people whose rights under certain statutes or regulations were being violated by state or local governments. For example, in Florida, the state welfare department, acting without any legislative authority to do so, required Medicaid patients to pay part of the purchase price for medicine. Legal-services attorneys challenged this rule, and the federal court halted enforcement.

In Maryland, legal-services attorneys sued the state to regain unemployment compensation for 24,000 Marylanders whose benefits were reduced through an erroneous interpretation of the law.

In Vermont, legal-services attorneys challenged Housing and Urban Development policies that resulted in tenant rentals in excess of maximum amounts allowed under federal statutes governing the Section 8 housing program.

These are not wild and irrational lawsuits brought by radical lawyers seeking to engineer social change. They are lawsuits that address examples of wrongful government policies and protect basic individual rights.

Critics of the corporation say that they want to return the legal-services program to local control. But under current arrangements, each legal-services project is governed by a board of directors composed of local people, 60 percent of whom are local attorneys and at least one third of whom are local low-income persons eligible for legal assistance. That *is* local control. The Reagan Administration seeks something very different; placing legal services in a block grant would sound a death knell for the program because many governors, like the former governor of California, would like the "troublesome" legal-services attorneys to disappear.

If the Legal Services Corporation is dismantled, government's promise to the disadvantaged of our country that someone will listen to their lawful grievances will have been broken. If that promise is broken, the consequences could be dire, for the whole society as well as for the poor.

"No law I have signed or will ever sign means more to the future of America." These were the words of President Johnson when he signed the Elementary and Secondary Education Act of 1965 (ESEA) into law, thereby fulfilling his pledge to make education "the first work of these times and the first work of our society." With such lofty goals, the federal government began its five-pronged effort to help educate poor children, to stock school libraries, to promote community-wide projects for educational change, to spur education research and development, and to upgrade state departments of education.

Now, a decade and a half later, American schools, particularly inner-city schools, still suffer from grave shortcomings. The litany of problems is familiar: thousands of functionally illiterate high school graduates; a decade of declining achievement-test scores; violence in the schools; labor strife and teacher layoffs; rebellion against taxes and bond issues necessary for schools to keep apace with inflation. These problems have been exacerbated in some communities by emotional and exhausting battles over school busing.

We stand at a crossroads with respect to the federal government's role in education. The path suggested by the Reagan Administration is to reduce sharply (and ultimately eliminate) federal support for public education. Not only do Reagan Administration officials see federal involvement in education as a waste of taxpayers' dollars but they imply that the federal role in education has had a highly destructive effect.

I reject that notion entirely. While not every ESEA program has been a resounding success, we have made remarkable progress in spotlighting children's needs and in providing a modest beginning to educational equality for all children in this country. In 1950, for example, only 50 percent of our young people graduated from high school. Today, that figure is 85 percent. The increase for black youths is even more dramatic. In 1960, only 20.1 percent of blacks aged twenty-five or older had completed four years of high school. By 1976, the figure had more than doubled, at 44 percent. From 1968 to 1978, black enrollment grew from 6.4 percent to more than 10 percent of all college students. The achievement reflected in these statistics is real, tangible, and commendable.

Substantial evidence suggests that federal funds, beyond giving access to education, have actually enhanced the learning experiences of children. Title I of ESEA is the primary program of federal assistance to our nation's elementary and secondary schoolchildren. It recognizes that children from low-income families are the ones most likely to be deprived of appropriate educational experiences, and that local educational agencies cannot bear the heavy costs required to meet their special educational needs. In 1977, the National Institute of Educational, the education-research arm of the government, conducted an extensive study of the Title I program. According to the institute's findings, Title I services make a distinct contribution to the learning of poor children. Detailed case studies of school districts receiving Title I funds revealed that "Title I students in every district received extra services—either more time in instruction, smaller group size, or more time with highly qualified teachers."

Perhaps the most encouraging accomplishment of Title I found by the institute is its effect on student achievement. The study indicated that first graders made average gains of thirteen months in reading and fourteen months in mathematics in the seven-month period between fall and spring testing. Third graders gained seven months in reading and fourteen months in mathematics. These gains are especially significant when one considers that without Title I, disadvantaged students usually have an average achievement gain of seven months per ten-month school year.

President Reagan says that he is not anti-education. He wants only to turn the responsibility for education back to the states, where it properly belongs. But we should remember that the federal government got involved in education in the first place because the state government and local school districts defaulted on their responsibility to try and educate all of our children to their full potential. In many states, malapportioned state legislatures averted their eyes and turned deaf ears to the desperate educational need of inner-city or minority children.

Reapportionment and the Voting Rights Act have increased the representativeness of many state legislatures and, to some extent, their sensitivity to urban problems. Unfortunately, at the same time, the states face some of the same pressures that burden the federal government. The affected cities must contend with a now-familiar but nevertheless desperate situation: the movement of middle-class families to the suburbs simultaneously eviscerates the cities' tax base and leaves the school systems heavily populated with the poor or minority children most in need of costly special-education services. Under these circumstances, the federal government's responsibility remains crucial, and the Reagan alternative becomes a cruel hoax, particularly when the administration seeks to cut federal aid to those school districts that are most in need while proposing to use federal tax revenues for tuition tax credits that only encourage middle- and upper-class men and women to remove their children from the public school system.

If the Reagan Administration intended to "fine tune" such programs as food stamps, legal services, and elementary and secondary education, I would be strongly supportive. If the Reagan Administration intended to rid the programs of fraud, waste, and abuse, I would be supportive. But, as I perceive it, this administration intends to destroy these programs and with them the whole notion of a federal responsibility to meet social needs. Fundamental principles of economic and social justice are at stake, and they are worth fighting for.

THE WAR ON THE POOR[3]

It sounded like a dry exercise in bookkeeping, a clerkly transfer of bureaucratic functions: "A financially equal swap." An exchange "with no winners and no losers." Those were the terms in which Ronald Reagan described to state legislators the centerpiece of his new federalism—a plan whereby the fifty states would take full responsibility for food stamps and welfare, and, in a fair exchange, Washington would take complete charge of Medicaid.

Similar assurances accompanied the proposed 1983 budget cuts in aid to the poor. "Don't be fooled by those who proclaim

[3] Magazine article by Nick Kotz. *The New Republic.* 186:18–23. Mr. 24, '82. Reprinted by permission. Copyright © 1982, The New Republic, Inc.

that spending cuts will deprive the elderly, the needy, the helpless," the President warned. What may appear to be budget reductions are really only part of "a slowdown in the rate of federal spending." In fact, he emphasized, the highest priority in his budget, along with national defense, is to redirect resources toward "a reliable safety net of social programs for those who have contributed and those who are in need."

However Mr. Reagan softens these two Presidential initiatives with his own aura of goodwill, one fact is still clear. Ronald Reagan's long-stated goal has been a dramatic dismantling of federal social welfare, shifting to the states the responsibility for the basic survival needs of the poor. And that is his aim, both in the 1983 budget cuts, and in his accompanying plan for turning Aid to Families with Dependent Children, food stamps, and dozens of other programs over to the states. To comprehend what the President is proposing, and to separate reality from rhetoric, one must focus on both the 1983 budget and the new federalism. Taken together, these Reagan proposals represent a radical revamping of national social policy. More than that, they represent an *abandonment* of the national social policy that has been evolving since the beginning of the New Deal half a century ago. As Senator Alan Cranston, Democrat of California, describes it, the Reagan program is "a prescription for abdicating our national commitment to meeting the most basic human needs of our poor, disabled, elderly citizens, and our children of tomorrow."

At the very least, the Reagan plans represent a clear rejection of a long-held Republican doctrine about social welfare: that it should be designed to help people help themselves, to encourage the work ethic, and to encourage an end to dependency. The Reagan budget cuts hit hardest at the so-called "working poor," those families whose breadwinners perform the least desirable jobs in American society at the lowest pay, are scraping by—toward the day they or their children can get ahead—only with the help of minimal government assistance. Buried under layers of myth about self-perpetuating welfare dependency is the fact that during the 1960s and 1970s hundreds of thousands of families *escaped* from poverty and the dole with the help of federal welfare, food, education, job training, and health programs.

The President's recommendations promise to have significant long-term consequences. If the budget cuts and social program transfers are adopted, if tax reductions go fully into effect as scheduled, and if the Pentagon budget increases are approved, it will take a generation to reorder sufficient taxes and revenues to return the nation to a more generous social policy.

In presenting his $755-billion budget, with its $91-billion deficit, the President stressed that it only slowed the growth rate of federal social spending. But the cuts set forth in the budget documents for fiscal year 1983 belie that statement as it applies to the major programs that serve the poor. These programs—ranging from AFDC and food stamps to training programs and low-income housing—would be slashed 18 percent from their present levels.

Most of these cuts come on top of earlier budget cuts recommended by Mr. Reagan and approved by Congress for 1982. And many are compounded by their interacting effect on the same poor people, thousands of whom benefit from a combination of federal aid programs. Millions of needy Americans, particularly the aged and working poor, would lose all their assistance or have it cut sharply.

Furthermore, grants in aid to the states are cut so sharply ($3.5 billion in 1982 and $9.8 billion in 1983) that governors are wondering how much would be left of programs which Mr. Reagan proposes "turning back" to the states. Governor James Thompson, Republican of Illinois, says of the new federalism, "The 1983 budget is absolutely critical to this whole thing." Governor Richard Snelling, Republican of Vermont and chairman of the National Governors' Association, adds: "These cuts would fall heavily on many of the nation's needy citizens and would shift unacceptable burdens to state and local governments already struggling with the recession and deep 1982 federal aid reductions." At their recent association meeting in Washington, the governors, with near unanimity, opposed the notion of the states' taking on AFDC and food stamps by declaring that their growth "has far outstripped increases in basic indicators of need" and has become "a major source of persistent deficits, excessive taxes, and of poor economic performance."

The government's own statistics and studies tell another story. These programs and others which primarily help poor people comprise only 7 to 10 percent of the budget, yet they have been singled out for far heavier cuts than any other government activity. As for "outstripping increases in basic indicators of need," the AFDC program is providing 24 percent less aid, adjusted for inflation, than it did in 1969. And the food stamp program, with its 43-cents-a-meal "thrifty diet," lags two years behind soaring increases in the cost of food. In contrast to the 18 percent cut in programs for the poor, the Reagan budget proposes only a 1.5 percent reduction in the $290-billion-a-year array of entitlement programs (Social Security, Medicare, veterans' disability, and military, civil service, and railroad retirement) primarily serving the non-poor.

This pattern has led to criticism like that of the *Miami Herald,* which charged in an editorial that the President is using the poor "as cannon fodder in a holy war against inflation and big government." Anticipating such attacks, the President advised Americans to ignore "horror stories about people who are going to be thrown out in the snow." But the stories abound, and they are not, as the President would like us to believe, fabrications. The results of the much less severe 1982 cuts can be seen at soup kitchens and other communal feeding centers throughout the country. At a food program for the elderly operated in a synagogue in northwest Washington, D.C., a worker notes an influx of elderly white people whose food stamps have been cut. They are using what meager cash they have to buy medicine. They can no longer afford enough food. Relief agencies throughout the country are reporting requests for assistance from a new kind of supplicant: intact families in which one or both breadwinners have lost their jobs, their supplemental food stamps, or AFDC assistance.

Those food programs that were created or expanded in the late 1960s and early 1970s—after it was discovered that millions of Americans, because they lacked sufficient income to buy food, suffered from malnutrition or outright hunger—have been singled out for particularly severe cuts. The 1983 Reagan budget calls for slashes in each of these programs, and the new federalism foresees elimination of a direct federal role in all of them except the school lunch program. A dozen different studies have credited these programs with dramatic reductions in hunger and malnutrition, and with contributing to improved health among the poor.

The Women, Infants and Children program, which provides $950 million for medically prescribed food aid supplements for two million women and young children who are at nutritional risk, would be eliminated. Its funding, reduced by more than a third, would be folded into a block grant in which the money could be used for other purposes. States, already hard-pressed financially, for the first time would have to match federal funds. At least 700,000 people would lose benefits in a program that has long waiting lists and a record which documents contributions to lower infant mortality and mental retardation, and to improve health.

The school breakfast and child care center feeding programs also would be eliminated, with their previous funding reduced by 50 percent and combined into a block grant to the states. These cuts in food aid would gouge even deeper into the programs in subsequent years, because funding would be frozen at $488 million. Hundreds of thousands of poor children would lose their free school breakfasts. Reductions would be sharper in child care center feeding, the losers being poor children and working mothers who depend on low-cost day care.

Proposed cuts in the food stamp program would eliminate benefits entirely for three million people and reduce aid for fifteen million others. Sixty percent of those losing benefits are members of families whose total income is already 50 percent below the government poverty line. The working poor, no longer permitted an 18 percent deduction for work expenses and taxes, would lose $2 out of every $5 in food stamp aid, an average yearly family loss of $684. A family earning $5,000 a year would end up receiving $400 less in food stamps than a family subsisting entirely on $5,000 a year in welfare. Senator Patrick Leahy, Democrat of Vermont and a member of the Senate nutrition subcommittee, notes that this kind of budget cutting encourages "people to stop working and go on welfare."

The elderly would lose $1 out of $4 in present benefits for an average annual loss of $192 per family. An elderly couple living on $425 a month in Social Security benefits would have its annual food stamp benefits reduced from $312 to $120. If these older people also were receiving $30 a month in fuel aid, their food stamps would be eliminated. And if they were living in government-assisted housing, their food stamp benefits, which will now be counted as income, could result in a sharp increase in rent.

Benefit losses are even more severe for families who had been living on earnings from minimum-wage jobs, supplemented by AFDC payments. In most states, 1982 budget cuts have already eliminated all AFDC support for a mother of three children who earns as much as $5,000 a year. These families also lost their eligibility for Medicaid. Many may now be better off financially by quitting their jobs or greatly reducing their working hours. The 1983 budget calls for eliminating the Work Incentive Training program, through which hundreds of thousands of AFDC recipients have received training and job placement. Instead, states can require welfare recipients to participate in "work-fare," earning their AFDC checks in unpaid work at public jobs.

Those measures are not the result of quirks in the budget-cutting process. President Reagan has advocated similar ideas for years, encouraged by Martin Anderson, until recently his chief domestic policy adviser, and by Robert B. Carleson, now his special assistant for policy development and formerly his state welfare director in California. These two longtime advisers share Reagan's view that programs which permit workers to receive welfare or food supplements are too expensive and philosophically unsound. Their approach is to make government assistance so scarce and so unattractive—low benefits and unpaid labor—that potential recipients will have no choice but to get by on whatever work is available at whatever wage. The President explained the idea recently: "If you start paying people to be poor, you are going to have a lot of poor people."

The new federalism represents an extension of the strategy of the budget cuts: shrink federal social welfare and then place responsibility with the states, where it is certain to shrink further. In addition to the swap—AFDC and food stamps to the states, Medicaid to the federal government—Washington would "turn back" to the states responsibility for forty federal programs in education, social services, community development, and transportation. To pay for them, the President would create a $28-billion "federalism trust fund," collected from federal excise taxes on alcohol, cigarettes, and telephone service, and one-half the federal tax on gasoline. When the trust fund and federal excise taxes are phased out in 1991, the states can enact their own excise taxes to pay for their new responsibilities. (Excise taxes, however, do not provide a reliable, growing source of revenue, since they are based on units sold, not cost. Such taxes are also far more regressive than the income tax, and they are hard for a state to enact—particularly if neighboring states do not.)

Under the sketchy proposal announced in the President's State of the Union message, and amplified somewhat since then, many crucial details are left unsettled. But the direction of the program is clear: welfare responsibilities would be given to the states to deal with as they see fit—if they see fit. As a practical matter, states would have great latitude in deciding the range of benefits, or whether to continue programs at all.

Reallocating government responsibilities within the federal system to achieve greater simplicity, efficiency, and accountability is an idea that has broad appeal. Disagreement arises over the all-important details. In President Reagan's view, the transfer of AFDC and welfare to the states "will make welfare less costly and more responsible to genuine need because it will be designed and administered closer to the grass roots and the people it serves." Governor Bruce Babbitt of Arizona, perhaps the most prominent Democratic advocate of giving the states wider latitude, disagrees. "These programs are properly a national responsibility," Mr. Babbitt says. "When the unemployment rate is 16 percent in Michigan, but only 5.5 percent in Texas, it is manifestly unfair to ask Michigan residents to shoulder welfare burdens created by national economic policies. The safety net ought to be fashioned as a matter of integrated national policy equally applicable to an elderly citizen or malnourished child whether he lives in Maine, Mississippi, or Arizona."

Philosophical differences aside, the evidence strongly suggests that the proposed exchange would not be a "financially equal swap with no winners and no losers." In theory, the federal government would be assuming about $16 billion of state Medicaid costs and the states would pick up a similar amount of federal AFDC and food stamp costs. But the dynamics of the new arrangement virtually guarantee that poor people will be losers. Both the state and federal governments will be drawn irresistibly toward cutting the benefits of all three programs now offered in most states. Any states that resist a reduction of benefits to the poor would almost immediately face higher costs than in the present arrangement.

The Reagan Administration has talked about "maintenance of effort" by the states, requiring them for at least several years to spend as much on food and welfare functions as was spent in the past. But this safeguard would offer only limited protection to the poor. At present, food stamps is a national program with uniform national standards, fully financed by the federal government but administered locally by the states. AFDC is a cooperative program, in which the individual states set their own entitlement standards, but the federal government pays 50 to 70 percent of the costs. Medicaid is a joint program, in which both the individual states and Washington have some voice in setting entitlement standards, and the federal government pays 50 to 70 percent of the costs. The key issue is what would happen to benefit levels and costs when states assumed full responsibility for food stamps and AFDC, and the federal government full responsibility for Medicaid.

With all its imperfections, the food stamp program today is the sturdiest safety net available to all needy Americans. In contrast to Social Security, AFDC, Medicaid, and veterans' benefits, the only qualification is need, defined by the national poverty line ($8,450 annual income for a nonfarm family of four, $5,690 for a couple). Benefits are available to the elderly, intact families, single parents with children, single persons, and couples without children. Uniform benefits are adjusted periodically to reflect the cost of living. The 21 million participants represent a broad cross section of the poor. Food stamp households have an average gross income of $325 a month; more than half have no liquid assets and half do not own a car.

Food stamps were expanded into this uniform, national program specifically because many states did not make the earlier program available to people in obvious need. As late as the early 1970s, hundreds of counties, including ones with the worst problems of poverty-related malnutrition, refused to operate programs. Other states provided inadequate benefits to only a small percentage of their poor. It is difficult to imagine how any state today would run a food stamp program on its own: printing and distributing its own stamps, authorizing and policing food stores, safeguarding stamps from counterfeiting, etc. For individual states to take on these responsibilities, now borne by the federal government, would involve prohibitive administrative costs and burdens. It seems inevitable that states would eliminate the food stamp program, and increase welfare checks to offset at least partially the loss of food stamps, for at least some of the present food stamp recipients. But then the states would run into a whole new set of difficult issues involving costs and welfare policy.

The vast majority of states, in their present AFDC welfare programs, exclude thousands of current food stamp recipients from eligibility. Half the states do not provide benefits to intact families, and none provides benefits to single people or childless couples. Furthermore, the AFDC benefit and eligibility levels in many states are far more restrictive than national standards of the food stamp program. A number of states provide benefits only to families at or below 50 percent of the poverty line. Unless states broadened their eligibility standards and raised their benefits, millions of persons now receiving food stamps would lose their food benefits and receive nothing in return.

According to President Reagan, the states are up to meeting this challenge, thanks to civil rights and reapportionment laws introduced over the past twenty years. Those laws have made profound differences, but a vast disparity remains between the national standards of food stamp aid, determined in the White House and Congress, and AFDC standards in the various states. In Mississippi, a mother and two children with no other income receive a maximum AFDC grant of $96 a month. In Texas, a family of four receives a maximum of $141—or $38 less than that oil-rich state paid in benefits 12 years ago. In Arizona, a family of four receives $224, based on a standard of need last updated 10 years ago. Twenty-two states provide maximum benefits of less than $285 a month (or less than 50 percent of the poverty line). Since 1970, only two states have increased benefits as much as the inflation rate, while more than half the states have failed to reflect even one half of the increase in the cost of living.

It is the food stamp program, with its single national standard of need and regular updating of benefits, which has helped ease the disparities among states. Since food stamp benefits are tied to income, recipients in states with low AFDC benefits—or low wage levels—receive more food stamps than do recipients in higher benefit states. To pick the most extreme example, in Mississippi, a family of four receives the rock-bottom AFDC payment of $120 a month, but gets $235 in food stamps. Beyond any question, the food stamp program has revolutionized the standard of living for the poorest people in that poorest of American states.

Even when the states are relieved of their Medicaid costs, there is little reason to suppose that many of them will extend welfare coverage or raise benefits and update them periodically to achieve the same level of coverage provided by a combination of AFDC and the federal food stamp program. In fact, the evidence suggests that the elimination of federal financial support will lead to a reduction in welfare benefits. At present, with Washington paying 50 to 70 percent of the costs, states have had some motivation to raise even the most inadequate ADFC benefits. With more popular and powerful constituencies competing for limited state resources, it is difficult to envision states raising benefits, which for the first time will be fully dependent on state funds.

Relinquishing the federal role in AFDC and food stamps could hurt the poor in other ways as well. The needy will lose federal procedural rights to apply for aid and to get a hearing before aid is cut off. These rights to benefits with a federal component have been developed painstakingly by Legal Services lawyers and advocates of the poor over the last twenty years. In the past, many states and local jurisdictions gave or withheld aid with little regard to fairness and few procedural safeguards for the poor.

The net effect of the AFDC and food stamp transfer to the states would likely be an evaporation of whatever semblance of national standards have been set by food stamps. More people will move from low-benefit states to those which provide more generously for the unemployed and the needy. President Reagan will have created a welfare system directly contrary to the system envisioned in the national welfare reform efforts of the Nixon Administration in the early 1970s. Back then, Ronald Reagan was one of the few governors who opposed national welfare reform; he was advocating the same states-centered approach he has introduced today.

Somewhat ironically, the federalization of Medicaid also is likely to result in a distinct pattern of "winners and losers." At present, Medicaid eligibility requirements and the level of services differ greatly among the states. Twenty states use their own widely varying AFDC eligibility standards for Medicaid as well. Thirty states permit participation by the "medically needy" who have slightly higher income. Some states provide for "optional services," such as prescription drugs, eyeglasses, and dental care, while others do not. If Medicaid is operated as an entirely federal program, it would seem inconceivable, and probably unconstitutional, for such differences to be permitted. The federal government could hardly operate a national program in which, as at present, a family of four in California can get Medicaid if its annual income is below $7,800, but a similar family in Arkansas qualifies only if its income is below $3,100.

If the federal government set national Medicaid eligibility standards and benefits at the level of the more generous states, such as California, New York, and Massachusetts, the total yearly cost of the program would rise by some $14 billion—an unlikely objective for the Reagan Administration. It is much more probable that some middling standard would be set, by which needy citizens would receive improved coverage in the most limited benefit states, but fewer benefits in the more generous states. If these higher-benefit states decided to supplement federal Medicaid, they might be big losers in the "financially equal swap."

In making his recommendations, the President invited his critics "to put up or shut up." The most logical response to his new federalism proposal would be a different kind of trade, one in which the federal government keeps food stamps and takes over Medicaid and/or AFDC, and the states assume responsibility for less basic kinds of aid. But this would not be an equal swap financially, nor would Mr. Reagan buy it. So the present prospect is for trench warfare over which budgets get cut how much, and how much of last year's tax bonanza stays on the books.

The biggest danger is that Mr. Reagan's planned destruction of basic support systems for the needy will be carried out in the same atmosphere of haste, public ignorance, lack of debate, and political expediency that surrounded last year's budget cuts. The poor no longer have a strong voice in Washington, as they did in the heyday of the civil rights and antipoverty movements. More than anything else, the poor need advocates who can effectively take their case to the public. As a recent Opinion Research Poll showed, 38 percent of the public put a high priority on cutting "welfare," but only 9 percent would cut "aid to the needy."

In off-the-cuff remarks in recent weeks, Mr. Reagan has continued to evoke a cheerful mythology about the problems of being poor in America. People who want to work can find pages of job openings listed in the newspapers. The hungry can eat by gleaning leftovers from the fields. Donations from food manufacturers can fill the gap. Poverty can be ended if each church would adopt ten families. Ronald Reagan has been purveying this kind of mythology, along with stories about the welfare queen from Chicago (his current example: the pupil who receives a free lunch and whose parents earn $72,000 a year), since his 1950s stint as a goodwill speaker for General Electric. Myths persist because people find it useful or comforting to spread them and believe them.

President Reagan wants to have policies that make poor people suffer, but he also wants to maintain his good-guy image. That is why, one recent day, he phoned a television anchorman to find how the federal government might help an elderly couple who had been shown losing their home because of an unpaid tax assessment. As it happens, it was a lawyer from the Legal Services program who had brought the couple's plight to the public attention, and is now fighting to save their home.

In the real world, one thing the President might do is reconsider his commitment to abolish that program. As the lawyer said, "I'm gratified he called and has compassion for them, but I'd like him to come down here and see how much misery his policies have caused."

URBAN ENTERPRISE FRAUD[4]

During a midsummer visit to Baltimore, President Reagan
had a vision which he said "reinspired" his faith in the doctrine
of the urban enterprise zone. He saw free enterprise thriving
amidst adversity. In the company of Mayor William Schaefer he
passed ten minutes chatting with the forty employees of the Commercial Credit bindery at the edge of the Park Heights ghetto. For
the rest of the morning Reagan told whoever was listening that
"we've seen a vision today of our cities, and it works." What
works, he repeated, was not direct federal funding to cities, which
his Administration has cut drastically, but private initiative. And
in order to stoke this powerful engine, he had proposed legislation
to establish enterprise zones, distressed areas in which tax and
perhaps regulatory concessions would be offered to persuade businesses to relocate or expand.

But the President, like the concept of enterprise zones, was
surrounded by contradictions. Mayor Schaefer indecorously ushered Mr. Reagan to a sign detailing the sustained government involvement that had made possible both the bindery and the Park
Circle Industrial Park in which it was located. The city prepared
the site with funds from the Commerce Department's Economic
Development Administration, which the Administration has abolished; made improvements with Community Development Block
Grant funds, which have been cut; paid a private developer to provide technical assistance with CETA funds, also cut; and has used
every possible revenue source a municipality can devise to attract
business with cheap loans and tax-exempt financing.

Faith, of course, clears the hurdle of contradiction effortlessly.
The zone had become a totem of the Reagan religion. It is removed
not only from the social reality which it is intended to address, but
also from the fairly modest and sensible ideas about tax incentives
and job creation of which it purportedly consists. The enterprise
zone is a piece of legislation, to be discussed and debated; but it

    [4] Magazine article by James Traub. *New Republic.* 187:11+. O. 18, '82. Reprinted by permission.
Copyright © 1982, The New Republic, Inc.

is also a free-floating political fantasy. The zone idea first surfaced in England in 1977, and two years later supply-side proselytizer Arthur Laffer brought it to the attention of Representative Jack Kemp. Already a firm believer in the value of tax cuts, Kemp saw the enterprise zone as a way of fostering entrepreneurial, job-creating activity in the most inhospitable surroundings, and recreating the golden age of the small businessman waging the good, clean fight of capitalism. Kemp's attempt to design a bill around the enterprise zone concept attracted the attention of Robert Garcia, a liberal Representative from that shoo-in zone qualifier, the South Bronx. Garcia had a different past in mind: the neighborly South Bronx where he grew up, and where his aunt, as he likes to tell listeners, worked, shopped, and lived all within a few blocks. For Kemp the zone means job creation; for Garcia, inner-city revitalization.

Over the course of the next year, the bill was modified by the suggestions of a wide range of interested parties, endorsed by candidate and then President Reagan, and altered once again to satisfy the new Administration. None of these changes was radical. What has been completely altered, however, is the context of the legislation. Under Carter the enterprise zone would have been one among many efforts by the federal government to rescue inner cities; under Reagan it has become an antidote to the ills supposedly produced by those very federal efforts.

As it stands now, the "Enterprise Zone Tax Act of 1982" offers several major tax breaks. Businesses that locate in the zone will receive a credit equal to 10 percent of their payroll. Employees will receive a credit equal to 5 percent of their wages—in order, as Kemp's staff aides explain, to make work more attractive than welfare. Businesses that employ "disadvantaged individuals" will receive a credit equal to 50 percent of the employee's wages for three years, and a declining fraction for the next four. Capital gains taxes will be dismissed altogether. Investment in new plant and equipment will receive a 10 percent credit over and above the current 10 percent credit.

There is no shortage of reasons why these incentives are not likely to induce any businesses, or any of the right businesses, to locate in a slum, or to expand if already there. The failure of last year's massive tax breaks to do anything more than feed the federal deficit casts doubt on their value as a form of economic policy. And the existence of these tax advantages makes yet another round of them marginally less valuable. But even if businesses do respond to changes in the tax law, studies have repeatedly demonstrated that they do not relocate because of them, and many businesses do not even avail themselves of the abatements with which cities and states try to tempt them. And if businesses *can* be bribed into relocating, will $6,000 or so per employee per year be enough to make them hire people who have never had a steady job? "I don't want a tax credit for hiring and training people if it's going to hassle me," says Dan Henson, adviser on minority-owned business to Baltimore's principal business association. "There's not that much tax incentive in the world."

And then there's the small-business problem. Kemp has been powerfully influenced by the discovery of M.I.T. economist David Birch that 80 percent of new jobs come from small business, and that these businesses are too small and too numerous, and fail too often, to expect to benefit from traditional "targeted" aid. Small business, in other words, will make the enterprise zone go, and changes in the tax law can reach those firms when increments in federal aid could not. But tax credits don't do any good unless you make a profit, and most small businesses, and all new ones, make little or no profit. They need money immediately, to get going or to stay alive. Kemp and Garcia originally made a number of the credits refundable, meaning that the Treasury would pay an amount equal to the credit to unprofitable firms. But the Administration eliminated these provisions.

A final point is that almost no one wholeheartedly supports enterprise zones except the Administration and Jack Kemp. Susanne Hiegel, a lobbyist for the National Conference of State Legislatures, describes the feelings of many of the group's members as "lukewarm." A National League of Cities meeting in April produced, according to the league's legislative analyst, William Barnes, "no general enthusiasm" for the bill. Many planners and specialists in the problems of cities denounce the idea outright. Even its proponents have lost some of their enthusiasm. An aide to Garcia explains that his boss supports the bill, in no small part, because "he knows that there's nothing else coming down the pike."

Still, you never know. Maybe it'll work. Nobody, after all, can point to received wisdom on urban policy with much pride. Transfer payments do create some harmful dependence, both by cities and individuals. Tax and regulatory burdens do make a difference to businessmen. And enterprise zones do appear to be relatively cheap—$300 million a year, according to a wild guess by the Treasury Department. That's only two-thirds of the entire appropriation for the popular Urban Development Action Grants for 1982. Jack Kemp thus offered to a Senate committee the most persuasive argument for the zones. "Should enterprise zones not succeed, we would be no worse off than before."

This noble conception has been comprehensively detailed in the 28-page background document that accompanied the President's enterprise zone bill. The document opens with a ritual castigation of "the old approach"—"massively bureaucratic" and profligate—and a brief sketch of the new approach. A primary recommendation for the enterprise zone is thus highlighted in boldface type—"No Appropriations."

After a discussion of the tax breaks, the document moves on to another bee in the Reagan bonnet—regulation. Though its fervor was moderated by the need for liberal support, the Administration still included in the background document suggestions that state governments "revise or abolish" occupational licensure laws and usury laws. As Susanne Hiegel says, "How would you feel if a barber came at your throat with a straight razor" and no license? How would you feel if you had to pay 40 percent interest on your credit card or car loan?

Critics of the zone idea have pointed out that devastated areas are tough places to do business, and the Administration has agreed that improved local services are essential. But no direct federal grants will be forthcoming, and with the reduced federal commitment, cities will not be able to add much to a strained budget. So the answer is ending the "government monopoly" on municipal services. While some limited experiments have shown that the private sector can pick up garbage more efficiently than a city and that community groups can do better at managing day-care centers, the Administration suggests that practically everything short of public safety could be turned over to the private sector in zone areas. Perhaps the private sector could pay teachers less to get them to locate in the South Bronx.

This vision of a stateless utopia in the ghetto, with "large shopping crowds" attracted by a "potential boom," is capped by an un-Republican peroration to the virtues of community control. The Administration's background documents close with a detailed description of Neighborhood Enterprise Associations. These NEAS would issue Class A and Class B stock, thus transforming a slum into a joint-stock company. They will take over virtually all functions of government. They will "rebuild communal social structures and value systems." They will "serve as focal points for voluntary, self-help efforts by the zone residents and others." They will establish "little league teams" and "scout groups." Right there in the ghetto.

Back in the real world, Baltimore is busy proving that the urban policy that the Democrats left behind can be used to great advantage. Baltimore hasn't missed out on a federal program in a quarter of a century, but it has learned to absorb them with the active involvement of the Mayor's office, the private sector, and community groups. Driving down Baltimore's Pennsylvania Avenue, you can see the enormous, glum housing projects of the 1950s on the one side, the spruce, small-scale public housing with lawns and fences on the other. In the Ridgely's Delight neighborhood, not far from the famed Harborplace, you can see tidy brick townhouses built for low-income families with the Section 8 funding that the Administration has cut to the bone, mingled with fine houses that prosperous young professionals bought for a dollar in a state of decay and rehabilitated at their own cost. You can see crowded markets rebuilt with Community Development funds.

In Park Circle, President Reagan's road to Damascus, nobody doubts the value of public funds. None of Baltimore's five industrial parks would exist at all were it not for Mayor Schaefer's remarkable abilities as a raider of the federal treasury. Mayor Schaefer likes to refer to Park Circle as an "enterprise zone" to show that Baltimore is in tune with Washington, but the incentives it offers are in the $5.5 million of federal, state, and city funds which Baltimore has used to buy land and improve the site.

Of the four firms now doing business in Park Circle, only the smallest, Mom's Chicken, has gotten there on its own. Its owner, "Slim" Butler, thinks he may have enough of a profit to benefit from tax credits. Harold Bereson, the owner of Cindarn Plastics next door, has stayed afloat with a loan from the Small Business Administration, and is certain that the tax provisions of the enterprise zone bill can't help him. Frederick Barrett, of United Sounds of America, is preoccupied with trying to find a loan to finance his fledgling business. He expects five years to pass before he turns a profit. Only Commercial Credit can expect to benefit significantly from the tax breaks. President Reagan's instance of noble entrepreneurship happens to be a public-spirited venture by the giant Control Data firm.

Frederick Barrett was hoping that the President would visit him so that he could tell him what he thought of enterprise zones, not to mention abandoning the poor. Barrett, who is black, is a registered Republican and the first executive director of the Consumer Product Safety Commission. His $4,500-FM tuner has been voted the finest such product in the world by *Stereo Magazine* in Japan. His faith in free enterprise is fervent. An enterprise zone, he says, will do little for Park Circle without start-up capital and additional funding for infrastructre, security, and counseling—"and that's not going to come from private business or anywhere else." To Barrett, the zone, shorn of the other tools of economic development, is "like you build a six-lane highway through Appalachia, past the mountains, and then you stop right in the middle." A suitable judgment—likening the enterprise zone to one of the ill-considered and above all utopian projects of the 1960s.

THE DESPERATE PLIGHT OF THE UNDERCLASS[5]

Concern about unemployment and poverty in the United States is rising. In simpler times business managers might have observed sympathetically and increased charitable giving without feeling any direct responsibility to understand or solve those problems. But the times are not simple, and nearly everyone is expecting business not only to act but to lead.

Millions of Americans are looking for jobs, and other millions who could be employed have given up the search. Our concern in this article is with a particular segment of the poor and the unemployed: the 10 million people in desolate neighborhoods of our major cities who are either more or less permanently poor or unemployed, those who have been called the "underclass." Disproportionately black, Hispanic, and young—although by no means exclusively so—the underclass is composed of single mothers, high school dropouts, drug addicts, and street criminals.

For this group either welfare or crime has become the only way of life. Its members live in disintegrated communities, cut off from the legitimate economy, the world of work, and political power. They are alienated, traumatized, angry, and hopeless. Moreover, having fallen out of the reach of schools and job training programs, they face little opportunity for permanent employment and often see little hope for improving their lot.

President Reagan has invited American business to address their problems. Last October, he challenged the National Alliance of Business to help those who were "economically trapped in welfare" and who "don't know how to free themselves." Suggesting that government antipoverty programs had done more harm than good, he asked for "private sector leadership and responsibility for solving public needs." And he announced the formation of a 44-member task force to take on the job. Led by recently retired

[5] Magazine article by George C. Lodge, professor of business administration at the Harvard Business School, and William R. Glass, associates fellow at the Harvard Business School. *Harvard Business Review.* p 60–71. Jl./Ag. '82. Reprinted by permission of the Harvard Business Review. Copyright © 1982 by the President and Fellows of Harvard College; all rights reserved.

Armco Steel chairman C. William Verity, Jr., the task force is composed of leaders from corporations, foundations, volunteer groups, and religious organizations.

The president thus pinned his hopes for social improvement on private institutions; but he provided no specific suggestions about what each group should do, how cooperation between such disparate sectors could be achieved, where funding for the effort would come from, or what role federal, state, and local governments should play in helping to "foster a greater public-private partnership."

To get some sense of the problem and of how they plan to respond to the president's call, during the last several months we have interviewed a number of leaders in business, in government, and in a variety of nonprofit and community development organizations. We found a good deal of bewilderment and uncertainty. We have reviewed various efforts that are under way to address the problems of urban disintegration and the underclass. Our purpose here is to offer some suggestions for determining what works and what doesn't and for deciding how business can help.

The Situation

Ever since the war on poverty was declared in the mid-1960s, substantial federal funds have been directed toward its elimination. A welter of federal programs had dealt out cash and in-kind payments to those in the lowest income categories. While helping to fill basic needs, such programs and funds have not reduced crime, violence, unemployment, drug addiction, or inner-city instability.

Those are the symptoms of a different and perhaps more insidious aspect of poverty—the poverty of alienation. The social, economic, political, and spiritual ties between the underclass and the rest of society have weakened or severed. The combination of broken families, lack of skills, unemployment, and crime creates a nearly unsurmountable barrier to entry into the mainstream community. With no access to the rewards of that community, the underclass feels none of its responsibilities. For them, there is no American dream, no sense of social membership, only hopelessness and ultimately despair.

The flow of federal transfer payments to the poor and to the welfare economy it has produced has in many ways increased the isolation of the underclass and its abandonment by other social sectors. While supplying basic needs, welfare programs have also created dependencies that discourage initiative, disintegrate families, erode discipline and self-respect, remove the motivation for education, and foster a burgeoning criminal economy. Furthermore, such programs have relieved other institutions of a sense of responsibility for the underclass.

The reduction of government spending at all levels may decrease the size of the underclass by forcing some to jump the widening gap into the mainstream economy. But unless the gap is reduced and avenues of mobility are opened, those who are close to the reality of urban disintegration expect that many will move naturally to violence and crime. Already, crime has an aura of heroism for urban youth, who see drugs, vandalism, and arson as a way to avoid the degradation of welfare-induced idleness and to gain power, prestige, and income.

Harry Spence, the court-appointed receiver of the bankrupt Boston Housing Authority (BHA), described the conditions facing the underclass in that city: "The issue is not poverty. The real issue is social membership. People can live poor if they have some sense of participation and membership in the larger community. It is the sense of isolation and total abandonment that produces violence." As employers have left Boston, residents of public housing have lost their jobs. (In some BHA projects up to 80 percent of the residents who could be employed are not.) Other institutions—unions, political parties, churches—have followed business out. Today, 4,000 Boston public housing units stand vacant, they are uninhabitable derelict shells.

At the same time, economic pressures are forcing more and more people to seek housing assistance. Already, 10 percent of Boston's population lives in government-financed housing. Another 7,000 persons are on the waiting lists. Rents, which are set at 25 percent of the residents' income, do not pay even the operating costs and leave nothing for rehabilitation or new construction.

Spence maintains that the only long-term solution to the problem is to restore a sense of community to BHA neighborhoods: "It is pointless for some company to come in here with jobs unless at the same time the district attorney's office, the police, and the municipality in general start to focus on these neighborhoods. A public-private partnership is essential."

The Approach

If business is to help the underclass gain full membership in American society, it can do so only by participating in efforts and organizations that bring together the prerequisites for the job— that is, a cooperative, holistic approach; the competence necessary; and acceptable authority.

The task is to build a sense of community where there is none, to reweave the severed strands of trust and confidence, to build a sense of participation in the larger community. Effective change can come about only by attacking the environmental circle on a wide arc, by using the solution of one problem and the establishment of one tie to solve and establish others. This change can only happen if several groups work together, each in its own area of expertise. Large corporations can provide jobs and management resources but must depend on school systems to train potential workers in basic skills, on churches and social agencies to help alleviate the family problems that interfere with work performance, on local government to provide police protection and city services for a safe, functional environment, and on small business entrepreneurs to bring needed commercial services to large companies and their employees.

There must be *competence*—that is, a collection of the skills, resources, capabilities, and understanding needed for penetrating the circle of problems effectively. Any organization or combination of organizations that would achieve change must have the ability to select, and be trusted by the disparate members of the underclass, some of whom are more unreachable than others.

To act as a change agent, any organization must be able to establish communication and other links with those who are outside the range of traditional institutions. But to complete the tie, it must also bring access to the resources of those institutions, including jobs, training, political influence, and funds from the government and the private sector. Besides the ability to bring the two groups together, competence also requires the ability to produce the level of confidence and motivation on both sides that is necessary for organization, disciplined activity, and new commitment.

There must be *authority*—that is, a decision-making process acceptable to all participants for setting the goals of community change, for determining the course and speed to be followed, and for making the trade-offs inherent in any change effort. The introduction of permanent and irreversible change into disintegrated urban communities is as much a political and social process as it is an economic one. Any change or opening of an additional access point, however slight it may seem, will threaten the status quo. Existing power holders will worry that change will erode influence, and those who are convinced that any change is threatening will feel anxious and afraid.

Attempts to alter the situation of the underclass raise questions of rights and legitimacy. By what right does a company or other organization presume to change a community? In whose interest and at what speed are the changes occurring? According to what criteria are the costs and benefits weighed?

The ability to decide these questions is rooted in the authority, or legitimacy, of the organization undertaking the change. Government is the normal source of community authority, but the residents of many disintegrated urban communities do not recognize the decision-making authority of even local government. Such communities have a void in authority; others have pseudo-governmental groups, ranging from indigenous religious organizations to youth gangs that function as the sources of authority. Any successful effort to bring change must include a legitimate authority to make the necessary decisions that those on both sides of the new links being established recognize. The experience of the KLH Corporation, makers of stereo equipment in Cambridge, Massachusetts, illustrates the need for an appropriate combination of competence and authority. In the late 1960s the company established a day-care center to meet the needs of its work force, which was largely minority women from nearby poor communities. Imbued with a sense of social responsibility, KLH management sought the best advice and assistance available from local universities. The result was often described as one of the most innovative child-care centers in the country.

Nevertheless, the parents of the children who attended the center protested that despite the good quality of the school, university researchers had no right to choose what was taught to their children. The KLH parents argued that only they had that authority, and they threatened to close the school. Management later agreed that the parents should supervise the school's activities. The protests ceased, and the center continues to provide day-care of high quality for the children of KLH employees. In this case, as in many others, experts had the competence but not the authority to solve a problem.

Job training is an example of using authority without the necessary competence. In 1981, the federal government spent more than $6.5 billion on job training, but few of the trainees ended up with permanent jobs. Most of the expenditure provided nothing more than temporary income maintenance. The failure to involve business adequately in the program and to employ its essential competence meant waste and disappointment.

What's Being Done

Numerous efforts are under way, and many organizations exist to deal with the plight of the underclass. In this section we will present examples of five types of organizations that we believe contain all the ingredients for bringing about change in disintegrated urban communities.

NEIGHBORHOOD ORGANIZATIONS

Throughout the deteriorated neighborhoods of America's cities are numerous small grassroots, self-help, private, nonprofit, and religious organizations that are endeavoring to improve the lives of the underclass and to restore their hope for the future. As Robert Woodson, American Enterprise Institute's specialist in community development, said, "These communities are filled with entrepreneurial talent—small businesses, neighborhood groups. We've got to figure out how to help them. They are the fabric of these communities. A lot of programs emphasize money and technology, but they don't tie into the social fabric that can improve the level of civility in the community."

United South End Settlements in Boston is an example of a successful local neighborhood organization. USES had its origins in the settlement house movement of the last century, when it was established to help new immigrants adapt to American life, but it has survived and evolved over time as the composition of the neighborhood has changed. Today, USES runs a variety of programs ranging from day-care for the children of working parents to the provision of low-cost hot meals to elderly neighborhood residents. Its multipurpose building is available to other neighborhood organizations and provides a popular resource center for social, educational, and cultural activities. Just over half of the USES budget comes from state and federal government sources. Director Frieda Garcia sees the cutback in federal funds producing even more pressure on private donors as the organization struggles to maintain its activities:

"We have always pinched our pennies to get the most out of the dollars we had, and we will continue to do that. But we are also going to have to try new approaches. I plan to analyze neighborhood employers to find workers who can pay full price for our day-care. I've also joined the Boston Chamber of Commerce to gain access to the business community. We can use its help in many ways, including its advice on running our food operation and engineering tips on making our building energy efficient. But our ability to reach out to them is limited by time and resource constraints, which are getting tighter."

Such community and neighborhood organizations, having sprung up in the environment of urban disintegration, clearly have competence and authority within the communities in which they operate. Their competence and authority rarely extend outside those communities, however, to the larger society, where they could achieve favorable regulatory treatment, government support, or access to a broad marketplace for their products. To serve as effective bridges for the underclass, neighborhood organizations need other institutions to reach out to.

FUNDS-CHANNELING ORGANIZATIONS

The Local Initiatives Support Corporation (LISC) is an organization founded to direct corporate resources toward grass-roots neighborhood organizations. LISC began three years ago in New York City with $5 million in seed money from the Ford Foundation and an equal amount from private corporations. Today its budget has grown to $30 million, and it supports numerous chapters around the country. A board of private, nonprofit, and community leaders direct LISC in each locality in which it operates. It serves as an intermediary, directing funds raised from the private sector to support the development activities of local organizations.

The LISC concept had its genesis in the experience the Ford Foundation gained by trying to improve conditions in the inner cities after the urban riots of the 1960s. As Mitchell Sviridoff, LISC president, said, "Out of that experience, it became clear that there is no one strategy, no comprehensive strategy that makes any sense. The most that anyone can hope to accomplish is incremental gain. Maybe if the strategy were well managed, one could stop the spiral of deterioration and reverse it—but this cannot be done overnight."

Consequently, LISC is structured to raise corporate funds and direct them toward efforts where they will have maximum impact. Again, in Sviridoff's words. "The only intelligent strategy now is an economic one that will make the most of the available resources in the community and build on existing strengths."

LISC operated by packaging its funds and making them available in the form of grants and loans to well-established local organizations involved in development projects. According to Sviridoff, "Community development corporations and neighborhood organizations have proved effective in arresting deterioration, reversing the process, and starting growth and development. They have also proved to be the best way of developing competent leadership and management of developing programs. A great many things have to be done if the process of deterioration is to be interrupted and reversed. There are difficult political choices, which no city management or private business can make, that only a locally based community development organization can make."

As an example of such difficult political decisions, Sviridoff cited public housing: "The selection of who lives and who does not live in newly constructed subsidized housing becomes absolutely critical. If such housing is totally populated by female heads of household and large numbers of pathological family units, it won't be good housing for long. There is no one who can control the selection or the eviction process more effectively than a neighborhood organization. Unless you can control who does and who doesn't live in newly constructed or rehabilitated units, you are doomed."

By working only with local organizations, LISC buys into authority that has been achieved and furnishes the resources to make the development process effective. Necessary competence comes from three sources: street-wise leadership within the community development organization, access to the larger community's resources through the LISC staff, and liaison with private corporations and nonprofit foundations for funds and other resources such as jobs and training.

By serving as an intermediary, LISC assists its corporate clients and boosts the development process through local organizations. As a conduit for corporate funds aimed at community revitalization, a specialist like LISC is much better than the companies at placing corporate community development funds, and its quality control over the recipients ensures maximum impact for the expenditure.

Cautiously optimistic about the potential for intermediary organizations, Sviridoff believes that more funds will be forthcoming once corporations realize that the monies are being used effectively. The whole process, though, is limited by the amount of funds large companies can set aside for community development. Even a doubling of corporate contributions to the community development process would replace only a small percentage of the cuts being made in the federal social budget programs.

FEDERALLY SPONSORED COOPERATIVE EFFORTS

Private Industry Councils (PICs) were established under the Comprehensive Employment and Training Act during the Carter administration. The purpose of the act was to provide employment and job training for the unemployed, and the objective of the PICs was to ensure private industry input into the design and structure of government-funded job training programs. Although most observers consider only a dozen or so exemplary, PICs now exist in 450 communities. Directed by boards composed of leaders from the public, community, and private sectors, PICs engage in activites centering on issues of business development, training, and employment.

Ted Small, president of the New York City PIC and chairman of the National Association of Private Industry Councils, outlines their mission as the provision of training that will allow those without marketable job skills to obtain permanent, well-paying jobs. The New York City PIC seeks to identify job categories in the private sector that have shortages of employment candidates. The PIC then either starts up or contracts for a training program in which its unemployed clients can enroll.

Government funds supplement wages during the training process and the initial period of employment; in return, private employers guarantee the graduates jobs. For corporations that have their own training programs, PIC provides pre-job training (instructions on punctuality, dress, on-the-job behavior) and then lobbies the companies to give its clients access to training spots.

Small cited the example of skilled machinists as one of his organization's successes. Through a survey of industrial activities in New York City, the PIC discovered that small manufacturing companies were turning down business because of a shortage of skilled machinists. With the advice of the potential employers, the PIC set up the only machinist training program in New York and has succeeded in placing formerly unemployed men and women in skilled, high-wage, long-term jobs while at the same time providing the scarce resources necessary for many small New York machining and manufacturing businesses to expand. Small says that numerous jobs are waiting to be filled and that many persons are looking for jobs; the bottleneck is that the applicants lack training in the skills necessary for the jobs.

Cay Stratton, executive director of the Boston PIC, agrees that government-sponsored organizations such as PICs can provide needed assistance to private companies. Through its business assistance program, the Boston PIC devotes a large share of its resources to alerting companies to available government help and thereby expands job opportunities for the unemployed. According to Stratton, "If you start coupling tax incentives with employment training, you are really talking about fairly hefty savings on the wage side. In many cases, savings have been dramatic. Many companies simply don't have any idea of the availability of this."

Stratton emphasizes that input from the private sector is necessary if cooperative efforts are to achieve their goals: "We have little to show for the great amounts of federal money poured into public service employment. That kind of experience never led to jobs in the private sector. Unless employers have a large share in the design and the management of training programs as well as in providing jobs, we don't do very well."

Government has the responsibility of providing the funds, while business offers experience and competence. The training programs run by the New York City PIC are ideal examples of this kind of public-private cooperation. The trainees prepare for jobs that are guaranteed by private employers and therefore fulfill a market need. Employers design training programs so that PIC trainees will acquire the desired skills. Public agencies have the authority and responsibility to select and help subsidize the candidates until they reach entry-level productivity.

John Filer, chairman of Aetna Life and Casualty and chairman of the National Alliance of Business, has encouraged both Aetna and NAB to "support, develop, and improve the operation of the PICs." They offer a widespread, cooperative structure on the community level that is already in place. In many communities, even where programs are regarded as less than outstanding, PIC board meetings provide a rare opportunity for business, government, and community leaders to meet in an atmosphere of cooperation. This is a requisite first step toward the multisector effort necessary to reintegrate depressed urban neighborhoods into the larger community.

Enlightened business leadership on PIC boards can give this type of organization an important role in providing avenues for the underclass to escape their status. But there is concern that the reductions in federal funds may greatly dampen such efforts. For 1982, Congress has cut the budget for the 450 PICs by 7 percent.

SEMIGOVERNMENTAL DEVELOPMENT ORGANIZATIONS

The South Bronx Development Organization Inc., like similar organizations in Baltimore, Philadelphia, Cleveland, Chicago, Newark, and other cities, is a nonprofit public corporation created to plan and manage the development of a disintegrated urban area. SBDO has received some $2.5 million of federal and state monies supplemented by foundation and project grants.

Although largely independent of city government, SBDO derives its authority from a board of directors whose members represent city hall, the State of New York, the Bronx borough president, and the six South Bronx community boards. By bringing in funds, jobs, services, and other resources, it serves as an intermediary between the residents of the South Bronx and the world of private and nonprofit organizations that are tying to bring new life to this battered 20-square mile area where 500,000 people live.

SBDO's achievements thus far have been modest but significant. It raised $110,000 from the Vincent Astor Foundation and the International Ladies Garment Workers Union to plan a 21.5-acre industrial park and nearby housing. The project, Bathgate Industrial Park, is well under way, the first building having been completed and fully leased. The Port Authority of New York and New Jersey has committed itself to developing the next three blocks.

SBDO contracted with City Venture Corporation (a consortium jointly owned by Control Data with several other companies and two national religious organizations) to explore the feasibility of setting up a technical assistance center for small businesses. SBDO then worked closely with the New York City PIC to develop training programs linked to job placement and economic development programs and secured the help of Avco Corporation of Los Angeles to conduct a Job Corps youth training program. SBDO also works with LISC in its efforts to invigorate local community groups.

SBDO and development corporations like it are an attempt to employ a holistic approach and to assemble the necessary combination of competence and authority to achieve community change. It does comprehensive development planning on an areawide basis. It provides, organizes, and contracts for competence from outside sources. It legitimizes the application of this competence through political ties both outside and inside the target area.

The creation of a development corporation tied closely to but independent of local government is an appealing way to ensure continuity through political changes in city hall. Particularly in municipalities where election cycles inevitably lead to program changes, an independent development corporation dedicated to community revitalization can be an especially good way to involve business in the process.

DIRECT CORPORATE INTERVENTION

Many corporations have attacked the problems of the underclass through unilateral action. Most of these efforts have taken the form of charity or extending regular business activities into poor inner-city neighborhoods. This philanthropy represents the provision of resources to others who have the authority and competence to use them for community revitalization.

A number of other corporations have tailored their operations to tackle community problems directly: IBM has built a plant in the Bedford-Stuyvesant area of New York City; Wang Laboratories has built in Lawrence, Massachusetts; Honeywell has pioneered in training and employing the handicapped; Chemical Bank has been making a special effort to hire the underprivileged in entry-level positions; Aetna and Prudential have allocated a portion of their investment funds to community development ventures that involve high risk.

Still other organizations, such as Clorox, Kaiser Aluminum, Bank of America, Security Pacific Bank in California, Hallmark in Kansas City, Procter & Gamble in Cincinnati, and the Minnesota Business Partnership in Minneapolis-St. Paul are recognized nationwide as leaders in the communities in which they operate. Most of these efforts are applications of a single special competence (constructing a manufacturing facility, hiring employees, making investments) in a traditional business area where the company's authority is widely recognized.

Two businesses make a practice of holistic community development. One is the Rouse Company, which has become well known for its success in turning decaying downtown warehouse and industrial districts into thriving commercial centers in Boston, Baltimore, and Philadelphia. The other is Control Data, which through City Venture Corporation revitalizes entire urban neighborhoods by planning and implementing industrial, commercial, and residential development.

City Venture operates in some ways like a community development corporation such as SBDO. It contracts with a city government or other local public authority to provide all or part of a comprehensive development plan for a particular neighborhood. It formulates the plan along with specific performance criteria, such as number of jobs to be created, and then contracts to implement the plan. By working with local community groups and bringing in outside resources, City Venture manages the development process. Like any contractor, City Venture expects to be held accountable for the performance goals it has set. It also expects to make a profit.

City Venture had its origin in Control Data's experience of building a factory in an economically depressed area of Minneapolis, an effort prompted by riots there in 1968. The company learned that normal practices had to be altered to establish the factory successfully. The company decided to hire employees on a first-come, first-served basis, to reduce a four-page application form to half a page, to set up a day-care center for employees' children, to make credit available to employees, and to teach its proper use. In all, bringing the Northside Minneapolis plant up to the employee training level of other plants cost $2.5 million. The government paid $1 million of that investment, and Control Data paid $1.5 million, which it regarded as the equivalent of research and development for a new product.

The eventual success of the Minneapolis factory led Control Data to repeat the effort in disintegrated neighborhoods of six other cities—in Toledo, Baltimore, Miami, Philadelphia, Charleston

(South Carolina), and Benton Harbor (Michigan). Each new factory was brought up to speed more quickly than the last until urban plant setups were on a par with those in suburban locations managed in more traditional ways.

Through these experiences, Control Data gained a great deal of knowledge about how to bring economic development to depressed urban neighborhoods. In an effort to make that knowledge generally available, Control Data used it as a basis for founding City Venture. According to Roger Wheeler, Control Data vice president, "There is far more learning necessary than I ever would have believed starting out on this path, nor do I believe most people understand what is necessary to make something like this work. It's like everything else; it's complex, and it's got a tremendous array of dynamics, many of which are out of your control. We've turned that learning into a product through City Venture."

Besides employing City Venture, urban economic development often creates a need for Control Data products such as its computer-based education system, its diagnostic health care systems, and its business and technology centers, where small businesses share support services.

Control Data chairman William Norris sees the response to social needs as his corporate strategy: "We started in 1967. We did not have all these products and services. If you get involved and your executives begin to see gain as prospective, then you will develop products and services as we did." He envisions the need for urban revitalization growing until there is massive public investment in it. He wants Control Data poised to take advantage of that investment.

Control Data's Wheeler recognizes that business alone does not have the authority to reshape communities but says that if it is frank about its objectives, a company can work with other groups to get the job done profitably: "There is a natural suspicion that a big company working in a community is going to rip it off. What Control Data has learned is that there is a process by which a partnership among community, government, and business can be formed and by which the answers emerge and emerge in ways that have a chance to bring about success."

Why Business Should Help

Each of the five nonprofit and community organizations we examined was operating prior to President Reagan's challenge to the private sector to help solve social problems. Each organization hopes business will translate increased interest and attention into increased support in the new environment. Each of the organizations furnishes at least one element of the public-private partnership necessary to establish the ties through which the underclass can rejoin the large society.

Optimism stems from the belief that corporations will join in efforts of the type just described and do the job. Pessimism, which is more prevalent, arises from the belief that business won't or that it won't know how. People also fear that government funds, which continue to be essential to any success, will no longer be available. For 1982, $22 billion has been dropped from social-budget funds, and another $22 billion in cuts is proposed for 1983.

Many business leaders argue that the primary responsibility of business in America today is to offer its goods and services efficiently and competitively. They say that the funds of steel, auto, and electronics companies, for example, should be invested in new plant and equipment to overcome our lost lead in the world economy. The best way to prevent an increase in the underclass is to provide new employment to the unemployed and increased income to the working poor. The leaders with whom we spoke, however, contend that economic growth alone will not solve the problems of the underclass. Though growth provides a context in which success is more likely, the problems of the underclass are structural, and extra effort is needed to reach them even with high rates of growth.

Most of the business leaders with whom we spoke believe that the problem of the underclass and the urban disintegration that its continued existence causes threaten the viability of American society. Large institutions such as banks, insurance companies, and retail stores cannot easily leave the cities where they are located. They depend on those cities for both a work force and a market, and being large, they are natural targets for violence. Consumer product manufacturers, too, find moving to healthier climates costly.

As John Filer has said, "If the city in which you do business
is in total disarray, it's going to be ever so much more difficult and
more expensive to operate your business in that community. People say, 'Well, I can always go to Houston.' Sure, that's fine, but
Houston in due course is going to deteriorate also unless we act."

Business leaders have a natural aversion to economic ineffi-
ciency. They argue that the cost of supporting the residents of disintegrated communities through income redistribution and repair
of the damage done by crime and violence is greater than the cost
of solving the problems. These leaders cite statistics showing that
the cost of creating a job and providing the training for a resident
of a depressed inner-city neighborhood is on the order of one-third
to one-half the savings that society enjoys by changing that person
from a net receiver of public welfare to a taxpayer.

According to Cay Stratton, "My numbers show that if you can
take somebody off welfare and train him or her within six months
to a year for a manufacturing job, that person will be making $6
to $10 an hour within the first two years, and you will get your
money back within a three- or four-year period. To train for
those jobs runs us, including a stipend, around $6,000 to $7,000
per person."

Another economic argument is based on an analysis of demographic trends and suggests that a company can directly benefit
from bringing jobs and training into inner-city neighborhoods.
Projections of future work force composition show a marked decrease in the number of workers in entry-level categories as people
from the baby boom mature at the end of the decade. As companies
compete for decreasing numbers of entry-level workers, they will
be forced to increase wages or to automate.

An alternative would be to find a new source of workers and
begin training now to guarantee an uninterrupted supply in the
future. The largest source of potential entry-level employees is unemployed youths in inner-city neighborhoods. Business will be
forced to train and hire them within ten years as the market ab-
sorbs other sources of labor. The company that learns how to tap
this labor market will have a competitive advantage. It can ensure
itself a steady stream of entry-level employees while its competitors are scrambling to fill the gap that demography promises. At

the same time that the company ensures its own future through provision of jobs and job training, the community benefits from reduced unemployment and the establishment of ties that provide inner-city youth with alternatives to lives of dependency or crime.

Some make a political argument in favor of business efforts to deal with the problems of community disintegration. By calling on American business to better the social system in this country and reduce the federal government's role in doing so, President Reagan has set high expectations for business performance. If business does not meet those expectations at least partially, and if people do not perceive an improvement, many business managers predict a severe backlash at the polls.

According to Roberto C. Goizueta, chairman of the board and chief executive officer of the Coca-Cola Company, "American business has one clear chance to prove that business unfettered will be business unflagging in service to American society. Today, we are beginning to get the opportunity that we have wanted for so long to prove that when private enterprise is relatively free, it can be the primary agent of response to human need. The Reagan administration has given us the chance to put up or shut up."

In the long term, community disintegration destabilizes the environment in which business operates. The presence of a large population cut off from the mainstream's economic and social institutions constitutes a threat to those institutions, especially within the confines of a city where the underclass forms a large percentage of the population. People can express unmet demands in a range of ways, from riots to support of "antibusiness" political candidates.

Most of the business managers with whom we spoke told us that their priority for government is to have it provide an environment in which they can operate their businesses efficiently. Now that the political environment is changing in a direction favorable to business, they hope to preserve the change over the long term by shouldering some responsibility for the structure and health of the society in which they operate.

Perhaps the most common response we heard to the question of why business should accept the president's challenge was that it is the right thing to do. Business managers want to be good citizens. They point with pride to efforts their companies have undertaken to improve their communities, not because they were in the companies' best interest but because they were the right things to do.

Though doing the right thing is a strong motivating factor, business managers also feel constrained in their freedom to allocate corporate resources to alleviate social problems. They complain of having few resources left after the claims of customers, suppliers, employees, and shareholders have been satisfied. Unless it is in the interest of the groups that make up the corporation, many managers despair of their ability to obtain the funds necessary for solving the problems of depressed urban neighborhoods even if they want to.

The Prerequisites

If business managers are to improvve the plight of the underclass by helping to build the bridges that will allow its members to reenter the larger society, there are some prerequisites for efficiency and effectiveness.

BUSINESS SHOULD NOT UNDERESTIMATE THE DIFFICULTY OF THE TASK

As Marcia Kaptur, former assistant director for urban affairs of President Carter's domestic policy staff, put it, "There is an enormous cultural gap between disintegrated communities and business. Business expects things to happen quickly; it wants clear measures of success. That's not the way things work in the inner city. Change takes a long, long time. Business must have great patience and not underestimate the challenge."

Effecting social change is not a market where returns come quickly or are easily measurable. Business managers who get involved in the effort must be careful to set realistic goals and maintain realistic expectations for themselves, their business colleagues, their cooperative partners from other sectors, and the persons they are trying to help.

Effective Action Requires a Large Corporate Commitment

If a company's goal is to achieve permanent change, it must expect to expend a large amount of resources over a long time. Those resources include both people and money. Several observers mentioned in our interviews that commitment to the effort by the CEO is a prerequisite for successful corporate participation. As John Filer put it, "I'm convinced that until the boss gets into this and understands it and you get it structured within the company, not much is going to happen. The resource commitment has to go beyond philanthropy. This isn't charity. This is business. You have to believe your survival depends on it."

The necessary human resources include those who have expertise in dealing with community groups, government agencies, and business's other partners in the community change effort. A corporation can obtain the necessary expertise either by expanding recruitment beyond traditional areas to bring it in-house or by working with such organizations as LISC and SBDO.

Corporations Must Have a Realistic Community Perspective

Although the economic access that business can provide to the underclass is of crucial importance, that tie alone is not sufficient to accomplish the goal of reintegration. A company that wants to contribute to community development must realize it is operating on only one plane of a multifaceted task. It is also necessary to ensure that the company's efforts fit into the network of relevant organizations—public and private—that we have described.

The introduction of small businesses into disintegrated communities should be an important component of the process. Before Congress now is legislation that would create enterprise zones providing incentives to encourage small businesses to locate in these communities. Without a holistic approach, however, such a program will fail. Unless the community, through both neighborhood organizations and local government, provides a wide range of services for a supportive environment, extremely vulnerable small businesses cannot survive. Large corporations, which serve as customers and advisers of small businesses, must also play a role in shaping the environment.

CORPORATIONS MUST COOPERATE WITH OTHER ORGANIZATIONS

To be successful, corporations must join organizations with similar goals. Business cannot make decisions alone. When initiating community development projects, where business managers can often play key roles, business must press for inclusion of other sectors. The five types of organization we have described all provide cooperative opportunities for business to become involved in the process of community change.

Such cooperation is not only beneficial to the community but also serves the direct interests of business. Companies need a pool of entry-level employees, which many business leaders complain the public school systems do not provide. Felix Rohatyn, chairman of the New York City Municipal Assistance corporation and a general partner at Lazard Fréres, has proposed a cooperative arrangement with mutual benefits:

"Inner-city school systems should be tied as directly as possible to employment opportunities, with the ultimate aim of being able to hold out the promise of a job if a child stays in school, off the streets, and out of trouble. The 'workfare' requirement being discussed by the present administration as a prerequisite for welfare payments should be replaced by a 'schoolfare' requirement. If job opportunities are created for inner-city youths graduating from school, a requirement for school attendance as part of the welfare program would be more meaningful than a requirement for menial and useless work."

BUSINESS MUST LEAD IN GUIDING THE FEDERAL GOVERNMENT'S

Since business is hard-pressed these days to keep alive and abreast of foreign competition, and since state and local governments are struggling to meet demands stimulated by federal budget cuts, the federal government continues to hold the key to success in eliminating the underclass in America.

Everyone with whom we spoke thinks that reducing the amount of federal management of the community development process and leaving much authority and responsibility at the local level would help put disintegrated communities back together. But all of them agree that the process cannot accelerate without federal funds. They are unanimous in their opinion that they have neither the resources nor the ability to take on the task of reintegrating the underclass alone. They complain about President Reagan raising expectations that private industry will replace the billions of dollars cut from federal social programs, while in fact the funds available to the private sector cannot come near doing so. While most are willing to increase their voluntary action, they feel that the federal government cannot abandon the task of either defining the goals or marshalling the resources.

As of this past spring, business leaders were openly expressing their worry that many of the federal cuts in education and welfare would only worsen the employment situation. By 1983, spending for disadvantaged students will drop 24 percent from the 1981 level as a result of decisions Congress has already made. In voicing concern about the administration's approach, Alexander B. Trowbridge, president of the National Association of Manufacturers, said he sees "no human resources policy per se." The confusion and uncertainty about federal policies in recent months has been almost as damaging to the organizations we examined as have the cuts themselves. SBDO, for example, was refunded in March only days before it was due to expire.

Though business cooperation in the types of efforts we have described can do much good, such efforts are on the micro level and can provide only small progress toward solving the overall problems. Business leaders must insist on federal policies that provide the necessary commitment over time in the form of funds, incentives, and guidance. If they do not, they will be saddled with blame for failure. The opportunities for business participation in the process of community development will have far greater chance of success and will in their sum help alleviate the larger problem if they are taken on in an environment of coherent federal policy that encourages wide participation and provides adequate resources.

If business leaders want to succeed in their efforts, they must help guide the federal government in the role it should play. To respond effectively to the president's call for help in solving our social ills, business must not only act but must lead in shaping the environment for its actions.

IV. THE FUTURE OF REAGANOMICS

EDITOR'S INTRODUCTION

So what is the future for Reaganomics? Almost no one seems to feel that Reagan's original plans for reshaping the Federal government can continue without some changes. One of the main forces for policy change is the spector of large Federal deficits. Reagan's tax cuts, combined with economic uncertainties and large increases in defense spending threaten to raise the budget deficit to unprecedentedly high levels.

Large deficits portend economic chaos, since the Federal government's need to borrow money inevitably causes a shortage of funds for other purposes and drives up interest rates.

Many economists believe that some kind of tax increase is necessary to decrease the deficit, and even some supply-side economists, who feel that tax rates in general should be lower, see the need for new taxes to close the budgetary gap.

John Oliver Wilson, Senior Vice-President and Chief Economist for the Bank of America, thinks that Reaganomics will survive if money is spent in the right ways. In a speech delivered in Los Angeles, Wilson urges cuts in defense spending and increases in government programs aimed at strengthening our industrial base. Otherwise, he fears that other countries will out invest us in this important area.

Seymour Zucker, an economist writing in *Business Week,* sees the new Reaganomics as more Keynesian than supply-side. He thinks that Reagan will turn now to stimulating consumer spending rather than continue to stimulate supply.

A review of Reaganomics in the *National Review* argues that Reagan has already abandoned Reaganomics. It sees the new taxes as Reagan's confession that he doesn't believe in his own economic pronouncements. According to this article, Reagan has surrendered to his democratic critics.

An article from *Fortune* by A.F. Ehrbar also notes moderating influences on Reagan's policies and a softening of the supply-side hard line. Ehrbar sees the deficits as Reagan's main stumbling block, and he thinks new taxes are acceptable as long as they are designed to minimize damage to economic growth.

John Kenneth Galbraith, Professor of Economics, emeritus, at Harvard University, considers supply-side economic theories to be fantasy. Writing in the *Harvard Business Review,* Galbraith argues for government control of consumer demand rather than an attempt to influence productivity. He also believes that in order to trim the Federal deficit, Reagan's tax cuts should be greatly modified.

The last words in this book are those of President Ronald Reagan. In a speech to the American people, Reagan argues for new taxes that are designed for "raising revenue from those who are not paying their fair share." He admits that these tax increases appear to run contrary to his policies, but he insists, they're necessary to trim Federal deficits. He adds that even with the new tax boosts, "the Federal Government will only be taking 19.6 percent of the G.N.P. (Gross National Product) by 1985."

CAN REAGANOMICS BE SALVAGED?[1]

Only eighteen months ago Reaganomics was born. It was an historic moment in our nation's history. Who can forget the dramatics of the event as it was broadcast live on nationwide television.

The date was February 18, 1981. President Ronald Reagan entered the packed Chamber of the House of Representatives to a thunderous standing ovation. As the members of Congress gathered to hear the new President lay out the details of his economic program, expectations were high, for rumors had been growing that this new program would represent a dramatic departure from the past.

[1] Address by John Oliver Wilson, senior vice president and chief economist for the Bank of America. *Vital Speeches of the Day.* 49:25-28. O. 15, '82. Reprinted by permission.

After first cautioning that "we can no longer procrastinate and hope that things will get better . . . they will not" the President went on to propose "a comprehensive four-point program."

It is a program, the President explained, that: First, is aimed at reducing the growth in government spending; second, reforming and eliminating regulations which are unnecessary and unproductive; third, encouraging a consistent monetary policy that reduces inflation; and fourth, reduces taxes.

It was the proposal to reduce taxes that became the most important part of the economic program. In his proposals for tax reductions, the President was far from conservative. Tax rates were to be cut by 30 percent. Tax revenues were to be reduced by $44 billion in 1982 and eventually result in a $500 billion reduction over the next five years. Never before in the history of the nation had a President proposed reducing taxes by so much for such a long period of time.

Drawing upon his prodigious abilities to communicate, and demonstrating an unexpected flair for playing the rough and tumble game of political arm-twisting in Washington, President Reagan moved quickly toward a vote in Congress on his tax bill. On July 29, 1981, after a mere seven hours of debate, the President won a land-slide victory.

As the newspapers reported: "In 190 days President Reagan has not only wrought a dramatic conservative shift in the nation's economic policies and the role of the Federal government in American life but he has also swept to a political mastery of Congress not seen since Lyndon B. Johnson."

It was now official. The accepted economic policy for the nation was christened: Supply-side economics. This new set of policies was expected to produce tremendous results. For 1982 projections were for an economy that would grow at a positive 5 percent real rate. Inflation would decline significantly, and the budget deficit would be a mere $45 billion. By 1984 the budget was to be totally in balance.

It seemed almost too good to be true. Massive tax reductions would stimulate such strong economic growth that sufficient tax revenues would be generated to balance the budget.

As all of us are only too painfully aware, this economic utopia has not occurred. There is little prospect that it will.

Rather than the economy expanding at a vigorous 5 percent, we find it declining at a negative 1.5 percent rate. Rather than a mere $45 billion deficit, we are faced with a massive $150 billion deficit. Rather than basking in economic euphoria, we are caught in the throes of the most serious economic recession in fifty years.

We clutch for every small indicator of economic improvement, knowing that unless we are on the verge of a protracted recession, or a depression, the economy should recover. There exist numerous self-corrective forces within our economy that act to turn a recession around. These forces are very powerful. A slowdown in inventory disinvestment and continued consumer spending are the most certain forces that typically act to turn around a recession. And it is just these forces that are operating today to give us what economic strength that we have.

However it is a weak economic recovery at best: *The weakest economic recovery in our entire postwar history!*

The seriousness of our current economic situation cannot be underestimated. In the economic debris of this recession we will be left with a frightening legacy: The *highest* unemployment rate since 1941 . . . the *largest* number of business bankruptcies since 1932 . . . the *weakest* recovery in business investment in forty years.

There is the very real possibility that such debris will simply overwhelm the expected economic recovery, and we will face a continued and prolonged economic recession.

In the President's own words, "we can no longer procrastinate and hope that things will get better."

Why is the economy in such dire straights? What happened to turn the euphoria of the Reagan economic program into pessimism?

Let us look at these questions. Specifically, let us look at two major issues: First, why has supply-side economics failed? And second, what can be done to salvage Reaganomics?

I separate Reaganomics from supply-side economics, for there are strong indications that the President is no longer wedded to his initial supply-side beliefs. Even more important, if Reaganomics is to survive, it must be separated from those beliefs.

Supply-side economics as advocated in the early days of the Reagan Administration has come apart for several reasons:

One: Overly optimistic assumptions were made regarding the role of expectations in our economy.

Two: The clash between expansionary fiscal policy and tight monetary policy, and the resultant rise in interest rates, was underestimated.

Three: The main engine for economic growth was assumed to be business investment; however, the impact on investment of high interest rates, a recession, and basic structural change was ignored.

Four: The impact of disinflation on the financial position of corporations was not taken into account.

Now, let's examine these reasons for the failure of supply-side economics in more detail.

First, overly optimistic assumptions were made regarding the role of expectations in our economy.

The role of expectations in our economy has become a major topic among economists in recent years. It is well known that past rates of inflation help form expectations about future rates of inflation. And it is generally felt that changes in economic policies have a significant impact on economic behavior. But what is not known is how fast inflationary expectations change and economic behavior is altered. The supply-side economists of the Reagan Administration assumed a very rapid response.

It was assumed that there would be a very rapid reaction to the announced economic policies of the new Administration.

Inflation would decline from then existing levels of 11 percent to 6 percent or less within a matter of months.

Business investment would be strongly stimulated by the mere passage of the economic program, long before the actual economic incentives had time to take effect.

Workers and consumers would begin to respond immediately to the new tax incentives designed to encourage greater work effort and a higher level of savings.

So strong would be the response to the new economic program that the Administration projected economic growth rising to 5 percent and inflation declining to 6 percent for 1982, while most private sector economists, using more conservative and traditional assumptions on the role of expectations, projected growth at 2.5 percent and inflation of 8 percent for the year.

In retrospect, it is clear that the Administration was much too optimistic in estimating the impact of expectations.

The second reason for the failure of supply-side economics was the clash between expansionary fiscal policy and tight monetary policy.

Once the President had signed into law his historic tax cut program, he set out to prepare his first budget. This was the budget that was presented to Congress in January, 1982. It was here that serious problems began to surface.

The President proposed massive increases in defense spending, $44 billion in FY 1983 alone, and against the strong recommendation of his advisers, he refused to accept sufficient tax increases to attain a more reasonable budget balance. Having run out of areas where social programs could be reduced, the Administration was faced with a budget deficit of $150 billion in 1982. And rather than achieve a balanced budget by 1984, the deficit was projected to continue to be $150 billion.

Such strong fiscal stimulus, unprecedented in our entire history, left the Federal Reserve Bank with no choice but to pursue a restrictive monetary policy. The result was an increase in interest rates. After having dropped by 600 basis points in the aftermath of the initial Reagan euphoria, short term rates soared by 400 basis points between December, 1981, and February, 1982. This was the period when the financial markets clearly perceived the true implications of the Reagan economic program.

As we know, interest rates have remained stuck at these high levels until July of this year, even though inflation was significantly declining and the economy was plunged into a serious recession. The markets simply were unwilling to move until the Administration faced up to the reality of their proposed budget deficits, and the Administration showed no signs of compromise as they engaged in a head-to-head confrontation with Congress.

It was only after the seriousness of the recession was finally acknowledged, and the intractableness of the financial markets was understood, that the Administration and Congress reached agreement on a proposed tax increase. But by then, the damage to the economy, and supply-side economics, had been done.

The third reason for the failure of supply-side economics was the assumption that business investment would provide the main source of renewed growth.

Unfortunately, rather than increasing, business investment declined. Little investment occurred when interest rates surged upward. Then when the recession occurred, and idle capacity began to develop, there was no need for new investment. But more important, business is faced with an uncertain future; a future of massive structural change and intense competition.

There have been few times in our history when our basic industries have gone through such significant change. My own business, the financial industry, for instance, faces the most dramatic change in over 50 years. We face intense competition from abroad as foreign banks enter American markets in increasing numbers. At the same time such nonbanking institutions as Sears, Merrill Lynch and others are broadening into financial services. Our costs have increased manyfold as we now pay market rates of interest for our source of funds. The risks of the banking business have grown substantially.

What is true of the banking industry is also true for airlines, automobiles, steel, computers, construction, agriculture, and aerospace.

At a time of such massive structural change in nearly all of our most basic and important industries, it was rather naive of the supply-side economic plan to place so much emphasis on a strong renewal of business investment.

The fourth area where the Administration miscalculated was in the impact of disinflation on the financial position of corporations.

During the past decade of high inflation, American corporations greatly altered their behavior. Debt financing was substituted for equity financing. Short-term debt was substituted for long-term debt. Capital investments were made assuming continued high inflation. Expectations about future income and profits were increased. Above all, borrowing was greatly expanded. All of these changes were normal reactions to a high inflation era. However, these actions created tremendous problems for all of us when disinflation occurred in 1982.

With the decline in inflation, the prices of products also dropped. Furthermore, many of your industries were locked into labor contracts where the cost of labor declined less rapidly than prices, and debt obligations where interest rates remained high. Consequently your business firms have been faced with declining prices but continued high cost for labor, interest payments on debt, and other fixed costs. The result has been a tremendous squeeze on corporate profits.

To counter this profit squeeze, firms have been scaling back on their investment plans. They have greatly cut all controllable expenses and delayed research and development activities. At the same time they were forced to continue borrowing at high interest rates in order to survive.

When the history of the 1982 recession is written, the most unusual occurrence will probably be the impact of disinflation on corporate financial strength. And this impact was almost totally excluded from consideration in the Reagan economic program.

Having discussed what has brought about the failure of supply-side economics, we now turn to the more interesting—and relevant—question of what can be done. Can Reaganomics be salvaged?

My answer is yes, for the Administration has many pluses working for it.

The first plus is the American economy. Our economy is still by far the largest in the world, accounting for one-quarter of the total gross national product of the global economy. This means that our markets are large and rich. We still offer the greatest economic opportunity for any manufacturer or entrepreneur in the world, whether that individual be American, Japanese or French.

The second plus is that we have absorbed the postwar baby boom into our labor force, thus we no longer face this problem that slowed down our productivity growth during the nineteen-seventies.

The third plus is that we have completed much of our investment in cleaning up our environment, another source of slower growth in productivity. We can maintain our commitment to a clean environment with far less resources than in the past, and now allocate those resources to other areas.

The fourth plus is the fact that the OPEC shock, which ushered in the era of high energy costs, is behind us, and we are well on our way towards adjusting to a more energy efficient future.

These pluses are so strong that the decade of the nineteen-eighties holds out the promise of potential growth rates in productivity that are two to three times that of the past decade.

However to realize this potential growth we must alter our current economic policies. Specifically these policies must be designed to expand investment in America's future.

This may seem a strange recommendation to make since the Reagan economic program was largely sold to business and to the public on its ability to increase productive investment. Indeed it was viewed as the most pro-business economic program in many years.

Unfortunately, it has put American business in its most precarious financial position in fifty years. It has stifled *private* investment. It has slashed *public* investment in housing, education, research and development, alternative energy sources, and public transportation. It is jeopardizing our future.

What needs to be done?

The first policy change would be to reduce the expected budget deficits. No one would suggest that we should attempt to balance the budget this year. To do so would only plunge the economy into a depression. Now it may not be possible, or even desirable, to reach a budget balance in the foreseeable future. But to consciously undertake policies that are designed to produce budget deficits of $100 to $150 billion from now until at least 1985, long after the economy will presumably be recovered from this recession, is to ask for trouble.

The second policy change would be to achieve greater balance between fiscal policy and monetary policy.

Smaller budget deficits are essential to achieving this balance. Once the proposed budget deficits are attained, the FED will be in a position to moderately ease on the growth of the monetary base without endangering our long-run commitment to fighting inflation.

Currently the FED is attempting to expand the money supply, but with large budget deficits this is a risky undertaking. It is only because of the weakness of the economy that the FED is able to ease to the extent it has without setting off renewed inflationary expectations and higher interest rates.

The third policy change is to reduce proposed increases in defense spending.

The Reagan budget proposes to increase federal government outlays by $322 billion between 1981 and 1987. Two-thirds of this increase is earmarked for defense! Two out of every three additional dollars spent by the government between now and 1987 will go to defense. (The remaining amount is slated for social security and medicare-medicaid.)

The defense establishment and the elderly will receive every single dollar of proposed budget increases for the next six years. There will be no increases for research and development . . . no increases for education . . . none for energy, public transportation, natural resources, and housing.

It will be impossible to achieve a more balanced budget without reductions in the $204 billion increase planned for defense. We simply do not have enough social programs left to be cut. Nor will procedural reforms, such as constitutional amendments to require a balanced budget or changes in the budget procedure, solve the problem. The solution requires some difficult political decisions on budget priorities, which leads me to my final proposal for change.

The fourth policy change is to increase both private and public investment.

Almost all of the emphasis in the current economic policy debate has focused on private investment. But private investment, by itself, will be insufficient to do the job. We need stronger and better public investment as well.

Unfortunately this is the area that has received the sharpest budget reductions. If we examine proposed budget outlays for the next five years in terms of four major categories: Defense, income security and health, general government operating expenditures, and public investment, we find that the only area where large reductions are proposed is public investment.

Defense is slated to increase from 24 percent of our budget in 1981 to 37 percent in 1987. Income transfer programs such as social security, medicaid and medicare will remain constant at 47 percent of the total. The cost of operating government, including interest on the debt, will remain constant at around 15 percent of the total. But public investment will decline from 16 percent of the budget outlays in 1981 to just 6 percent in 1987. We will reduce outlays on public investment by nearly one-half.

This is a high cost to pay.

At a time when our major competitors—the Japanese, Germans, French and other industrialized nations—are increasing their public investment, we are reducing ours. At a time when they have programs for strengthening their industrial base, we have none. We need more investment in research and technology, new developments in energy and computers, and a better educated labor force—not less.

We must face the fact that for the overall economic health and security of this nation, we must take a careful look at our expenditure priorities. We must achieve a better balance between fiscal policy and monetary policy. We must increase both our private and public investment: We must invest in our future.

While these policy changes are not politically popular, Congress and the White House have no choice. If our political leaders do their job, and we voters support them in their task, I am confident that Reaganomics will survive. But more important than Reaganomics, I am confident that our economy will survive.

Thank you.

REAGANOMICS II: MORE KEYNES THAN LAFFER[2]

Almost daily, some new statistic brings the heartening news that the U.S. is staging a strong recovery. Most economists are raising their forecasts, and some are saying that first-quarter growth could hit 6 percent. Does that mean Reaganomics is beginning to pass muster or that the economy's performance in the

[2] Magazine article by Seymour Zucker. Reprinted from the Mr. 21, 1983 issue of *Business Week* by special permission. Copyright © by McGraw-Hill, Inc. All rights reserved.

months ahead will be a good test of whether Reaganomics can deliver the sustained expansion that the President once promised for it?

The answer to both is no. Reaganomics as originally conceived and implemented is dead. What will now be put to the test is its successor, Reaganomics II—a policy that bears a striking resemblance to Keynesian economics.

Of course, Ronald Reagan, unlike Richard Nixon in 1971, is not about to declare, "I am now a Keynesian." Nevertheless, the policy coming from Washington these days is one that the Cambridge don would surely have embraced:

• Fiscal policy is highly stimulative. Even if the nation were at full employment, the budget would show a $91 billion deficit in the current fiscal year.

• Monetary policy is expansionary. The money supply has been growing at 16 percent for the past six months, and the Federal Reserve appears to be targeting interest rates once again.

• The Administration is pushing a $4 billion employment bill. The idea is to reduce long-term unemployment that will not readily respond to fiscal and monetary stimulus.

If the new Reaganomics does, indeed, deliver prosperity, it will not be supply-side guru Arthur B. Laffer who will be smiling, but the ghost of John Maynard Keynes. The old Reaganomics was built on three pillars: a huge tax cut—not to spur demand but to stimulate the supply-side of the economy through increased incentives to work, save, and invest; a tight monetary policy to fight inflation; and the idea of rational expectations, which said that the public interprets tight money to mean that inflation is headed down, so as money was tightened, interest rates would actually fall, not rise.

The fall in government tax revenues, argued proponents of the old Reaganomics, would be offset by increased revenues from fast economic growth. The pillars, however, turned out to be weak reeds. Government revenues began to decline, the deficit ballooned, interest rates rose, and the economy fizzled.

The new Reaganomics no longer talks about stimulating supply. It sees the problem of the economy as the same one that Keynes saw in the 1930s: inadequate demand. At a press confer-

ence on Feb. 25, President Reagan's top economist, Martin Feldstein, chairman of the Council of Economic Advisers, was asked
why, in view of big federal deficits, the third year of the tax cut,
scheduled for July 1, should not be canceled. His answer: "It
would take $35 billion at an annual rate out of consumers' pockets
and out of the spending stream. . . . The deficit would tend to
come down if we had a smaller tax cut, but in terms of actual ag-
gregate demand in 1983, demand would be lower." Treasury Secretary Donald T. Regan on more than one occasion has voiced the
hope that consumers will go out and spend their tax-cut money,
not save it.

Stimulus and Restraint

Keynesian economics performed poorly in the late 1960s and
even worse in the 1970s. Fiscal and monetary stimulus pumped
up the economy, but with it came inflation. Indeed, it appeared
that the point at which inflation started to boil over became progressively lower. So what Keynesian policy came down to was
stimulus—which had to be followed by restraint to contain inflation.

Yet this time there is reason to believe that the Keynesian demand stimulus of the Reagan Administration may work without
igniting inflation. What really wrecked Keynesian economics in
the past decade was OPEC. The twelvefold increase in oil prices
fueled inflation even as overall demand was falling. Now, food and
oil prices are declining. And consumer inflation in the first quarter
is expected to be about 2.5 percent at an annual rate, compared
with 6 percent last year and 10.2 percent in 1981. With a huge
oversupply in industrial capacity, prices could continue to moderate as demand picks up steam. Moreover, with lower inflation,
each dollar of the tax cut will go further in spurring spending. So
the economy will get more bang for each Keynesian buck.

Ronald Reagan's favorite President, judging by his fondness
for quoting him, is Franklin Delano Roosevelt. Ironically, in
1984, if Reagan has a good shot at capturing the White House for
a second term, it may be a result of the ideas of the very economist
whose theories 50 years ago formed the basis of Roosevelt's New
Deal.

REAGANOMICS WITHOUT REAGAN[3]

In July the Party of Compassion found a new hero. A Republican hero at that. He was Robert Dole, the Kansas Republican, Chairman of the Senate Finance Committee. The *New York Times* and the *Washington Post* eulogized him, and he was turning up on all the sober Sunday morning talk shows. Even George McGovern said admiringly that "Bob Dole has grown."

What had Dole done to win the hearts and minds of these liberal critics, so fiercely anti-Dole during the 1976 presidential campaign? He had merely steered through the Finance Committee a bill calling for what the *Post* termed "the largest tax increase in peacetime history." What's more, President Reagan backed Dole—tentatively at first, and then with the full weight of the White House. His chief advisor, James Baker, obliquely took credit for steering Reagan away from Reaganomics. He told an English interviewer that he was not compromising the President's anti-tax principles, "I'm simply adjusting them to realities."

Dole's warmest admirer, though, was *Time* magazine, which ran color photos of him in statesmanlike poses and echoed the theme that Bob Dole had grown: "They are not laughing so much at Bob Dole these days. . . . The difference now is that Dole's colleagues take him more seriously. . . . Dole has mellowed and matured . . . shunning rigid ideology . . . pulling Reagan and the White House toward a much needed package of selected tax increases . . . fending off New York Republican Congressman Jack Kemp and other unbending advocates of supply-side economics."

The Dole tax bill sailed through the Senate, even though not a single Democrat voted for it, either in committee or on the floor. Yet there were no hard feelings. In fact, Dan Rostenkowski,

[3] Magazine article by Joseph Sobran. *National Review.* 34:1074–1077. S. 3, '82. Copyright © 1982 by National Review, Inc. 150 E. 35 St. New York, N.Y. 10016. Reprinted with permission.

Chairman of the House Ways and Means Committee, said publicly, "Let's face it, Republicans wrote a tax bill that has been in the bottom drawers of Democratic tax reformers for years." The *Washington Post* thought Dole's bill richly deserved more Democratic backing. "Support the Finance Committee," urged an editorial the day after the Committee passed it. When the Senate passed it too, another editorial wondered innocently why Democrats were "cutting themselves out of any share of the well- deserved credit for the first significant move toward tax reform in decades." (Tax *cuts,* mind you, don't qualify as tax "reforms.") House Democrats appeared strangely eager to propel the bill unamended to the White House, letting Republicans hog all the credit.

Other odd things were going on. While applauding Dole's efforts to reduce the deficit by raising taxes, both the *Post* and the *Times* ran hysterical batches of editorials damning the proposed constitutional amendment to require a balanced budget every year.

It wasn't that the Party of Compassion was losing sleep over red ink. It was something else. Yet another *Post* editorial took the occasion of the Dole bill to sigh that Reaganomics, after an 18-month "fair trial," had, alas, failed. Was "discredited by events." Hadn't the supply-siders promised that the first whiff of tax cuts would spur an anticipatory recovery? And here we were, in a recession! Too bad.

Actually, as Paul Craig Roberts soon reminded the *Post,* only Martin Feldstein of Harvard had made any such suggestion. Orthodox supply-siders had predicted just the opposite: that investors would *defer* productive activity until taxes actually fell. The *Post* had still not managed, after 18 months, to grasp the supply-side case it was now dismissing. Clearly there was something other than empiricism at stake here.

But at least the *Post* had been elegiac about Reaganomics. The *New Republic* was less kind. It sneered that Dole and Reagan were "scared."

Less polemical press accounts are also being shaded to make Reagan, for once, the good guy: his old supply-side allies, meanwhile, are shown as acting out of "ideology" or even "theology."

Actually, of course, the supply-side approach is miles away from the old anti-welfare, budget-balancing fundamentalism of the Republican Party. But the Party of Compassion would much rather deal, right now, with the old fundamentalists, yea, even Dole.

In 1980 Ronald Reagan redefined the Republican Party. He made it seem more inclusive that it had previously appeared: a party for blue-collar workers and Catholics, not just bankers and farmers. Reagan's strategic pivot was the economy. He would use the supply-side approach, cutting taxes, rhetorically known as "getting government off the backs of the American people."

There are two levels here. One is narrow and practical, the other deeper and more philosophical.

Though often called a "theory," supply-side economics is common-sensical. It assumes that people work for rewards. If you tax them too much, you will not only discourage them but lower your own revenues.

Specifically, supply-siders say we are already overtaxed, and therefore it is in everyone's interest to lower taxes at least somewhat. By the same token it is irrational to go on taxing at our present rates.

The supply-side approach has been made to sound sectarian—"ideological"—but it was conceived as a pragmatic deal from the conservative side. It told liberals there was a community of interest in cutting taxes, and at the same time tacitly offered to pass up an overt fight over the principle of redistribution. All the liberals had to do was face—as many of them seemed ready to do—the natural limits of the welfare state. We would have lower tax rates, *and* more monies for existing programs; but, of course, no new programs.

That was all, but that was plenty. The Party of Compassion knew this meant, essentially, surrender. "Compassion," after all is a euphemism for a statist economy. By remote implication, our concern for our fellow citizens, even those totally unknown to us, should be limitless; and what is just as important, we should have faith that this concern can be mediated by a central government, through taxation and redistribution. (Wanting to hold on to your own earnings is, accordingly, "greed.") The state, in sum, is the locus of human community, and its policies should be framed on the assumption that we are all doggedly communitarian rather, than, say, "selfish."

So, from the liberal standpoint, the supply-side deal was nothing less than a trap: it subverted the great principle that the state's share of our income should increase, ratchet-like, indefinitely, approaching progressively what Arthur Okun used to call, with more candor than is common in those quarters, "equality in the distribution of incomes." Supply-side was a slippery slope to the jungle of laissez-faire. Nothing doing.

Liberalism, like politicized compassion, is an American variant of generically socialist positions. In Europe, men like McGovern, Edward Kennedy, Bill Moyers, Anthony Lewis, I. F. Stone, and so on would be frankly socialists or even Communists. Here they choose other designations, often saying they "reject labels" altogether. A wise ploy, though it really means they want to *control* the labels. They don't mind labeling their opponents: the liberals of yesteryear who haven't moved leftward have been re-labeled "neoconservatives" and accused of "moving to the right." The Party of Compassion never owns up to having moved leftward.

Because of his nice-guy approach, Reagan posed a real challenge. Some of his liberal critics during the campaign, led by Jimmy Carter, attacked him as a divisive force who would pit class against class, race against race, etc. But it didn't take, and in fact it backfired against Carter. Reagan came into office on a wave of good feeling.

The predominantly liberal press gave him a honeymoon for the first few weeks, as required by law. Reagan's niceness was the theme. To be sure, a note of irony crept in, as when Mark Antony kept repeating what an honorable sort old Brutus was. Were his *policies* all that nice? And was it very sensitive of him to wear thousand-dollar cowboy boots?

The feline corps, the blonde network White House correspondents, went to work on Nancy Reagan's wardrobe of expensive designer dresses. "Was she really," wondered Anne Taylor Fleming of CBS Radio's *Spectrum,* "a caring and compassionate person?" Especially with unemployment being so high and all. Then there was David Stockman, who was anything but nice. Lean and mean, he was ready for a fight to the death over "entitlements." Roger Wilkins, Mrs. Fleming's colleague on *Spectrum,* spoke for many when he called Stockman "a heartless young careerist."

But the compassion theme wasn't selling. During the budget battles of 1981, the networks hauled every available welfare mama, cancer victim, and eczema sufferer before the cameras to dramatize the results of Reagan's budget cuts. It was a pathetic ploy, and pretty soon "the Party of Compassion" got to be a joke even in *The New Republic.* The seismographic Paul Harvey spoke for millions, probably, when he told the networks to knock it off.

If compassion was out, the liberals still had a few cards left. A principal theme was that Reagan, however nice, had this "ideology" (conservatism), and this "untested theory" of supply-side economics, both of which would surely have to adapt to "reality" (the world as perceived by liberalism). The implication of all this bland cliché, the staple of the Sevareid set, was that Reagan and a few rootin'-tootin' New Rightists were the only ideologues in town. Reagan's critics, on the whole, were presumably pragmatists, moderates, realists. Nary an ideologue among 'em. (Nobody ever had to define the term *ideology.* Its function as a code-word was sufficient.)

Abruptly, in October, the Party got the break it needed—an almost incredible blunder by the young genius Stockman. He had been giving interviews—long, private ones—to William Greider of the *Post,* a master of sneer tactics. Stockman seemed to have conceded that supply-side economics was nothing more than a new guise for the "trickle-down theory" that if you feed the rich fat, the poor will get better leftovers.

When the interview, nicely twisted by Greider, appeared in *The Atlantic,* the liberals made a terrific uproar about it. To make things worse, or from the liberal point of view better, the fall economic indices showed that the nation had entered a recession. The economic mess that had greeted Reagan—double-digit inflation, high unemployment, higher interest rates—could now be laid entirely at Reagan's feet, just as the Democrats had learned to insinuate, at a similar phase of the Nixon Administration, that Nixon had started the Vietnam War. It was as if Reagan had caused every evil he had not yet cured.

On cue from Anthony Lewis of the *New York Times,* the Party quit talking about compassion and niceness and started talking about "greed." The gloves came off. The old leftist economist Robert Lekachman—who labels himself a "libertarian socialist"—produced the timely tract *Greed is Not Enough: Reaganomics.* Wherein he charged (and charged, and charged) that Reaganomics "enriches the already obscenely rich." This didn't exactly jibe with the Party's alternative theme that Wall Street had no confidence in Reaganomics; but it was in the general spirit of the campaign, so it was okay. Bill Moyers, Dan Rather's chaplain, intoned that Reagan's policies threatened to ignite a new class war. (Frances Fox Piven and Richard A. Cloward chimed in with a book titled *The New Class War.*) Morton Kondracke, in the *Wall Street Journal,* spoke of Reagan's "war on the poor." *Newsweek,* after a year of restraint, could bear it no longer, and ran a cover story titled "Reagan's America: And the Poor Get Poorer," with a piteous waif, her face smudged, staring dolefully at you. *The New Republic* howled of "huge transfers of wealth from the poor to the rich."

Again the implication of such talk passed unnoticed: all of it implied a zero-sum view of the economy, in which either the rich or the poor might do better, but not both. Reagan's view was precisely that *everyone* would do better if production were encouraged, and "rich" and "poor" would be comparative terms, not names of factions in a class war. The rhetoric of his critics, meanwhile, came straight from their own unacknowledged ideology, which was socialist.

For a man who is so often accused of making war on the poor, not to mention acting "bellicose" toward socialist countries, Reagan has been strangely subdued throughout. If he is going to make war, he might at least shoot back at his attackers once in a while. Or were they, when purring over his niceness, actually gloating over what they perceived as his weakness?

Maybe so. Though a brilliant politician, Reagan doesn't like to fight. He has been making conciliatory, not to say appeasing gestures toward the Party of Compassion from the start. Supply-side economics was foxy, but not, as Machiavelli would agree, leonine. Reagan was reluctant to force the real issue—socialism or capitalism—into the open.

He was eager to pacify the Party by appointing a woman to the Supreme Court. (Whether she has turned out as badly as the Right feared is, of course, another question.) Nancy Reagan was dispatched to strike warm, caring poses with schoolchildren. The President made a disarmament proposal in response to the nuclear-freeze movement, and leaped to prove he wasn't "racist" when he favored tax-exempt status for all private schools, yea, even all-white schools. ("Tax-exempt hate," snarled the *New York Times*, over and over again.)

The New Right particularly has worried from the start that Reagan would succumb to the softening-up process of liberal Washington's hermetic social and ideological pressures: the steamy vault that turns Republican crustaceans like Gerald Ford, John Anderson, and Bob Dole into soft-shelled crabs. Reagan, his private pollsters, and his advisors have all confirmed this apprehension with their own worries about the "sensitivity issue," which means simply that Reagan has assumed the burden of refuting his accusers. He has given his enemies full credit for good will: an ingenuous error, the error of a truly nice guy, but a disastrous error anyway.

Remarkable, this, because he came to Washington with a winning position—a position he had patiently forged. He had no real need to propitiate those who claim to speak for peace, equality, and baby seals even as they bare their teeth in sheer envy. Reagan also probably enjoys an enormous fund of latent sympathy among ordinary Americans who are sick of standing as defendants before their government, defendants, moreover, bearing the burden of proving that they are *not* racist, sexist, greedy, and lacking in compassion for snail darters. They know intuitively that in a free society the burden of proof should be on the accuser; which is to say, on the Left, whose position toward Middle America is hostile, censorious, and altogether accusatory.

Reagan should have rejected the charges outright and raised the issue of principle. The real debate *is* over principles, not motives, though liberals prefer to steer it in the other direction. The real question was never whether Reaganomics would simply "work." As Irving Kristol pointed out early in the game, the liberals were afraid not that it would fail, but that it would triumph.

It is baffling that Reagan has left the initiative to his enemies as he has. It is equally baffling that he chooses as advisors such veteran losers as Baker, the sort of old Republican whose weary conventional wisdom was refuted by Reagan's brilliant primary victories in 1980. When Baker says he is simply adjusting Reagan's views to "realities," he implies that he sees Reagan's views as somehow at odds with reality. And Reagan takes his advice! Really, it is as if Louis Armstrong hired a music teacher to help him blend into Lawrence Welk's orchestra. He was playing just fine by himself. One can only speculate that Reagan has lost confidence in his own greatest gift: his magnificent instinctive empathy with ordinary Americans.

If the game is going to be motive-hunting, the motive of the Left is now in full view: envy. *The New Republic,* in its rather tactless triumph over Dole and Reagan, forgot to mention the poor. Instead it jeered on and on about "the rich people's tax bonanza of 1981," "corporate lobbyists," "rich individuals," and "fat cats."

The real objection to supply-side economics is that it doesn't punish the rich. The liberal/socialist ideology holds that to hurt the rich is to help the poor—the class-war theory, you might say. Any reduction of tax rates is said to "favor the rich," so long as taxpayers with higher incomes get more money back, total, than those who earn less. This can only mean that the Left will exact, as the price of any tax cut, a sharp steepening of the graduated tax rate schedule.

But the Republicans' motives need some inspection too, and not the kind they have so far received. Dole justifies his tax bill in terms of "fairness," a concession to the Left. He speaks of it as a tax "reform." And when told that lobbyists opposing his bill were wearing Guccis, he quipped, "They'll be barefoot in the morning." No wonder Dole is a liberal hero—a "moderate," as he is now called. (A moderate being a Republican who resigns himself to the advance of socialism.) But why this sudden strain of anti-Guccism?

In his magisterial study *Envy: A Theory of Social Behavior,* Helmut Schoeck notes that in an age of mass politics, the fear of arousing envy can be as powerful a motive as envy itself. Liberal rhetoric about the rich has evidently gotten to both Dole and Reagan. There is something especially craven, though, about Dole's manner of joining forces with those he is appeasing, and snapping with assumed courage at the easiest targets in sight.

At first the Dole bill looked like a cinch. With Republicans capitulating to the cries that the deficit was getting out of hand, Democrats figured they could sit back and let their enemies self-immolate.

But of course the projections for the deficits ahead—and the $99.6 billion to be raised by Dole's bill—assumed precisely what supply-side economics denies, viz., that raising tax rates will not harm production, and that cutting those rates would lower revenues. This is the whole point at issue. For Reagan to accept the new tax increase as a device for closing the deficit is to confess that he doesn't believe in Reaganomics.

This was simply too much for many House Republicans. Led by Jack Kemp, 61 of them have written Reagan informing him that the new tax increase is "impossible to support." "Quietly, without debate," the letter reads, "the Republican Party is in danger of making a U-turn back to its familiar role of tax collector for Democratic spending programs." The Republicans also felt the Democrats had reneged on their half of the 1983 budget deal by refusing to make serious spending cuts.

So now the fight is on: the fight to save Reaganomics from Ronald Reagan. He is furious at the maverick Republicans, who have shown unexpected power. But Kemp reportedly told him in blunt terms that he knows of no economic principle that mandates, or even advises, raising taxes during a recession. The key, as Kemp is stressing, is capital formation. And Kemp argues that the Dole increase (the *Washington Post* now denies that what it once called "the greatest tax increase in peacetime history" even *is* an increase) would effectively wipe away whatever is left of the original Kemp-Roth tax-cutting program.

Kemp and Reagan are both on the line, but it is Kemp who has the strength of a powerful idea—an idea, moreover, bearing Reagan's own endorsement. The Dole bill may yet pass but only if Reagan, Dole, and the Democrats form a squirmy partnership, and are willing to take the heat of the continuing supply-side critique in the event that the tax increase deepens the recession. That will certainly give Reagan's advisors plenty of "realities" to improvise among.

In choosing to fight on terms chosen by the enemy, the Reagan team has turned the future over to the Democrats in the short run, and probably to Kemp over the long term. However the Dole tax increase fares in this session of Congress, the supply-side critique is here to stay. It will not lose its force because it happens to be momentarily outnumbered and abandoned.

If Reagan is angry, Dole himself is already on the defensive. He has now taken space in the *Post* to deny that he is a liberal, and to argue, however implausibly, that his bill is "consistent with conservative philosophy and supply-side theory."

Whether or not this is true, the Kemp revolt has forced Dole to justify himself in supply-side terms. It is depressing that Reagan and Dole, like so many "moderates," are angrier at the Right than at the liberals who have flummoxed them into their present mess. And yet it is Kemp who has caught the falling standard, and who has now ensured that the tax bill will be judged, with political consequences, from a genuinely conservative perspective. Whatever happens to the bill, that in itself is a victory. And whatever happens to Ronald Reagan, Reaganomics is here to stay.

REAGAN STEPS BACK FROM REAGANOMICS[4]

The transformation of Ronald Reagan, under way for many months, was detectable in his State of the Union address last week, particularly in the remark—good for a beaming ovation from Speaker of the House Thomas P. O'Neill—that "we who are in government must take the lead in restoring the economy." This from a man who used to say that government is the problem, not the cure. To be sure, the rest of the rhetoric sounded more like the old Reagan. It came across as though he were merely offering a

[4] Magazine article by A. F. Ehrbar. *Fortune.* 107:67+. F. 21, '83. Reprinted by permission.

few palms to the Democrats while still holding close to his original program. In fact, that rhetoric served to obscure a distinct pullback from the President's early objectives.

The centerpiece of Reagan's new program for taming the deficits is the tough-sounding "freeze" on federal outlays in fiscal 1984. Reagan hasn't really proposed holding 1984 spending at this year's level. Rather, outlays would increase by no more than the rate of inflation, so that "real" spending wouldn't rise at all. The Administration calculates that freezing real 1984 expenditures at the 1983 level will require cuts of $32 billion from the so-called baseline budget. The baseline budget is one that assumes no changes in existing programs, no new spending schemes, and the full amount of the President's originally scheduled buildup in defense outlays. Baseline spending for 1984 would be $880 billion, or nearly 3 percent more in inflation-adjusted dollars than this year's outlays.

Inflation-adjusted figures are the proper ones to use in evaluating government spending, and holding the line at zero growth certainly looks austere. From Congress's perspective, it's damned austere. But even a no-growth budget for 1984 is considerably fatter than what Reagan was promising two years ago. The frozen 1984 budget is nearly 16 percent higher, in real terms, than originally planned. The first Reagan budgets, unveiled in February 1981, called for annual *reductions* in the inflation-adjusted level of federal spending. By fiscal 1984 spending was supposed to be nearly 5 percent lower in real terms than it was back in 1981. But inflation-adjusted spending has gone up each year. (The last time outlays declined in real terms was fiscal 1970.) Even with the freeze, 1984 outlays would be about 10 percent higher in real terms than 1981's. *Fortune* calculates that Reagan is proposing $115 billion more in expenditures for next year than we would have had if he'd met his first targets for real spending.

Three forces came together to create that startling budget slippage. The recession, far deeper and much longer than predicted, pushed up expenditures for programs like unemployment insurance and welfare. Second, Reagan has stuck close to the dollar levels of defense outlays that he announced back in 1981. With inflation dropping much faster than expected, real defense spend-

ing shot up more than planned. Most important, at least in terms
of long-range budget impact, Reagan won fewer cuts in nondefense spending than he had figured on. The Administration never
even proposed all the nondefense cuts that OMB Director David
Stockman had factored into his early budget projections.

The 1984 budget might be viewed as Reagan's most ambitious
yet, since it finally would cut off the real rise in federal spending.
It certainly will be tough to sell politically. Even so, he hopes to
freeze expenditures at the high recession-fed level of 1983. Moreover, the President is asking for just one year in the cooler; expenditures get defrosted in 1985 and resume their upward climb.
Under the new long-range budget plan released this week, real expenditures will grow nearly as fast as the economy from 1985
through 1987.

Under the Administration's plan federal spending will drop
from more than 26 percent of GNP this year to around 24 percent
in 1984, but will still be over 23 percent after five years of economic recovery. Such distant forecasts of expenditures and economic
growth are notoriously unreliable, of course. And the Administration's economic assumptions have become newly cautious since
Martin Feldstein took over the Council of Economic Advisers.
The Administration's forecasts assume only 1.4 percent real
growth this calendar year and then 4 percent annual growth from
1984 through 1988. Nonetheless, two years ago Reagan said he
would reduce the relative size of the federal establishment to only
19 percent of GNP by 1984. Now he's saying that it could take
until 1989 or later just to get back down to the 22 percent of GNP
that he inherited from Jimmy Carter.

The $32 billion of spending "cuts" that Reagan wants in fiscal
1984 amount to less than 4 percent of the baseline budget for next
year. But even that modest reduction could be exceedingly difficult
to push through Congress, as Reagan acknowledges. The only
easy part will be the $8 billion that he has agreed to trim from
the $253 billion of baseline defense spending. Congress is eager
to cut even more from defense. The $8-billion saving would leave
a freeze-proof real increase of more than 8 percent in defense outlays, with warmer increases coming in 1985 and 1986. Reagan
said he'd propose $55 billion in defense savings over the next five

years. But the figure refers to reductions in budget "authority." The cuts in planned defense outlays, the amounts the government actually spends, come to only $47 billion over the five years.

Another $4 billion of Reagan's 1984 reductions comes from a six-month postponement, from July to January, in annual Social Security cost-of-living increases. The delay, part of a plan worked out by the bipartisan National Commission on Social Security and supported by both Reagan and Tip O'Neill, would save $40 billion in this decade.

Reagan hopes to achieve the remaining $20 billion or so of budget savings in other nondefense areas. Other benefits that are indexed to inflation, like veterans' disability and retirement pensions, would be subjected to the same six-month delay in cost-of-living increases as Social Security. Federal employees and pensioners wouldn't get any increases at all for 12 months. Reagan wants to freeze most spending on programs that lack build-in escalators at 1983 dollar levels, without allowing for inflation. And he says he will propose ways to finally throttle the runaway growth of entitlement programs (apart from Social Security). Reagan once again is stressing waste and abuse, and has singled out food stamps as a special problem.

That $20 billion of savings is a tougher goal than it first appears because it is net of the costs of new spending programs. These include additional school aid to the states, catastrophic-illness insurance for Medicare recipients, and added funds for unemployment relief. The President also wants more money to retrain displaced workers, and tax credits for companies that hire the long-term unemployed. Democrats and some Republicans in Congress want to do more.

Assuming that Reagan gets all the cuts he wants for 1984 (which he almost certainly will not), he'll still have to sell Congress on increasingly larger reductions from the baseline budgets for future years if he's to hold spending to 23 percent of GNP by 1988. Even if he succeeds, the savings may be barely enough to prevent future deficits from rising above the $208 billion now expected for fiscal 1983. To do better than that, Reagan would have to return to his budget-cutting ways of 1981 and slash away at both defense and what David Stockman once termed "the social pork barrel." The federal budget still contains tens of billions in programs that largely benefit business and the middle class, including regional development grants, revenue sharing, farm price supports, and subsidies to aviation, mass transit, and housing.

Without true austerity, which may be politically unfeasible in any event, material progress in reducing the deficits probably will require huge tax increases. The program that Reagan has laid out depends on tax hikes, though even attentive listeners to the State of the Union Address last week may be excused for failing to note that fact. Armed with a calculator and a sheaf of government documents, a listener might have figured out that in talking about the four-part plan "to increase economic growth and reduce the deficits," Reagan was proposing as much as $240 billion of tax increases—virtually all of a distinctly un-Reaganish variety. But the President mentioned neither the total figure nor the specific increases.

As explained by White House aides, the four-part plan would reduce prospective deficits by an impressive $558 billion over the next five years. However, that is the reduction from baseline deficits, not from the present deficit level. With all parts of the plan in place, deficits would still average $158 billion a year, or about $50 billion less than that expected in the current fiscal year. The total deficit reduction from 1984 through 1988 comes to $250 billion, just a little more than the tax increases.

The increases start with the Social Security rescue plan, which Reagan holds up as an example of the bipartisan cooperation needed to resolve the budget dilemma. Its principal element: $93 billion in new taxes during the 1980s. The total cost saving in this period is the $40 billion to be gained from the delay in cost-of-living adjustments. The agreement includes no other changes that will stem the growth of benefits. The added revenues will come from higher payroll taxes; higher taxes on self-employed persons; income taxes on half the benefits going to couples with incomes over $25,000 and individuals with incomes over $20,000; and payroll taxes on some of the people, like new federal employees, who don't pay them now.

The "fix" for Social Security will keep benefit checks going out on time, but that's all. The short-run solution loads most of the costs on workers and asks extremely little of beneficiaries, many of whom are better off than the people paying for benefits. And the plan does virtually nothing to solve the horrid financing crisis that is coming when the baby boom generation starts retiring 30 years from now. While politicians on all sides hail the compromise as a great achievement, many Social Security experts say it's a disaster. Many had seen the crisis as an opportunity to achieve such needed reforms as raising the retirement age for persons who are now in their 30s or younger and doing away with full cost-of-living adjustments for present as well as future beneficiaries who have incomes well above the poverty line.

The balance of the tax increases—$120 billion to $150 billion—is contained in what the Administration is calling a "deficit-reduction insurance policy." Reagan has proposed standby taxes equal to about 1 percent of GNP for the three years from fiscal 1986 through 1988, to take effect "only if absolutely necessary." Even if Reagan gets all the spending restraint he wants, and even if the economy grows one percentage point a year faster than he has assumed, the extra taxes will indeed be "absolutely necessary."

The specific levies under the standby plan include excise taxes on domestic and imported oil of $5 a barrel, or 12 cents per gallon of gasoline and heating oil, and an income-tax surcharge of around 5 percent on both individuals and corporations. Hardly anything could be more at odds with Reagan's basic economic policies than the surcharge and the Social Security tax hikes. The surcharge would negate about half the 10 percent tax cut, due this July, that Reagan has vowed to defend. The higher Social Security taxes will have similar anti-supply-side effects on after-tax incomes, and also will boost unemployment by raising labor costs.

The President's midterm prescriptions abound with other reversals and inconsistencies. After two years of reducing export subsidies, and amid heartening rhetoric about free trade, Reagan now plans to increase the loan-guarantee authority of the Export-Import Bank and may also authorize more direct lending to finance exports. Instead of reiterating his desire to abolish the Department of Education, Reagan has announced new block grants to states so that high schools can hire more math and science teachers. The old Reagan was more skeptical about feds in the class-room.

Reagan also proposes to foster investment in human capital by creating new tax-exempt savings accounts to help low- and mid-dle-income families meet college expenses. Apart from equity con-siderations (why should some households get more tax breaks on savings than others?), the plan flies in the face of Reagan's call for tax simplification. The Education Savings Accounts would confer the same tax savings as Individual Retirement Accounts, but would do so with a different set of rules. Tax credits for pri-vate-school tuition, which would vary with family income, would add yet another table to the tax form.

Just how far Reagan really has compromised his original ob-jectives won't be decipherable for some time yet. The sharpest re-versal, of course, is his advocacy of the standby, anti-supply-side surtax for 1986 through 1988. It could be that the impression Reagan created last week—that the surtax never will come to pass—reflects his true intent. Both Republicans and Democrats in Congress openly oppose the idea, and the proposal has virtually no chance of enactment in its present form. Knowing that, and also knowing that the remaining elements of his supply-side tax cut are in jeopardy, Reagan may have proposed the stand-by surtax purely as a political ploy to confuse his opponents.

The indexing of tax brackets for inflation, set to take effect next year, is in even greater danger than the 10 percent tax cut scheduled for July. Even some of Reagan's allies on Capitol Hill, including Senate Majority Leader Howard Baker, have been call-ing indexing an irresponsible giveaway that they'd like to repeal. Reagan seems to understand as well as anyone that indexing actu-ally is the most vital part of his first tax bill. If indexing is re-pealed, bracket creep could quickly wipe out Reagan's 25 percent tax rate reductions. Indeed, doing away with indexing could be a perverse way to enact a flat-rate tax. Without indexing, fairly rapid inflation could push virtually every worker into the 50 per-cent bracket by the mid-1990s.

Reagan, ever the optimist, may also believe that a supply-side miracle is on the way that will obviate the need for any new taxes. He rejects the increasingly popular notion that his supply-side nostrums actually contributed to the recession and are the principal cause of the gloomy deficit outlook. Economic logic is on the side of the President. Excessively tight money in 1981—much tighter than Reagan requested—is evidently what brought on the recession. And the failure to keep spending down to promised levels accounts for at least half of the prospective deficits, as the $115-billion spending overrun for 1984 shows.

Economic growth may well exceed the 4 percent rate that the Administration is assuming in its forecasts for the next five years, but it's hard to envision a boom big enough to tame the deficits. Administration projections show, for instance, that the deficit will be around $50 billion in 1988 even if growth exceeds the forecast rate by 1.33 percentage points a year. That calculation, which doesn't reflect revenues from the standby taxes, does include the rosy assumption that Congress will go along with every one of Reagan's spending cuts.

President Reagan has made a number of concessions to his liberal opponents in Congress. He has lowered his sights on spending cuts and accepted some minor reductions in his defense buildup. He has signed on to Social Security tax hikes that he must abhor and given his nominal endorsement to a partial repeal of the supply-side tax cuts. But he still hasn't come up with a budget that offers the certain prospect of declining deficits.

A truly credible plan for taming the deficits apparently will require more federal revenue, but business ought to urge that any increased taxes be designed to minimize damage to economic growth. A program that could work, and still keep faith with supply-side principles, lies in tax simplification. A major overhaul of both the personal and business tax codes, including abolishing scores of deductions and tax preferences, could generate substantial new revenues while allowing even further reductions in marginal tax rates, enhancing incentives to work and save. No tax is a good tax, but a properly crafted one is preferable to the fear and uncertainty caused by horrendous deficits.

THE WAY UP FROM REAGAN ECONOMICS[5]

A year or so ago, in the early days of the Reagan administration, I had occasion to give two lectures before business groups in Europe—one in Hamburg, the other in Zurich. Neither of my audiences could have been thought given to sentiment or wishful thinking; all present would have described themselves, not inaccurately, as typical hard-headed business executives. Yet I found myself encountering a measure of resistance to the argument I was offering.

I expressed doubt as to the efficacy of the supply-side economics then being proposed in Washington and urged that it would conflict with the severe monetary restraint also being proposed. This my audiences were most reluctant to accept. They did not wish to believe that an avowedly conservative administration, one supported extensively by American business, could be in error. They were unwilling, on the whole, to sacrifice their hopes for the reality.

I recall this experience not to affirm my superior wisdom. A stern and implacable god lies in wait for economists who reflect with approval on their past predictions; the future will even the score. Rather, I cite these wrong hopes as a prelude to urging against allowing political faith and hope to override business judgment in our time. Economic success or failure has little to do with ideology and nothing whatever to do with hope or even prayer. Policy can be good or bad under left or right, under liberal Democrats or conservative Republicans. Its requirements cut across political and party lines. That this is so is the first—and in some respects the most difficult—business lesson of our day.

It is my purpose here to apply this lesson to the deeper economic circumstances with which the industrial economies are now confronted. I also want to see if it is possible to go back of the headlines, the momentary comment, and identify the more fundamental forces that afflict current economic life and policy.

[5] Magazine article by John Kenneth Galbraith, Paul W. Warburg professor of economics, emeritus, Harvard University. *Harvard Business Review.* p 6–12. Jl./Ag. '82. Reprinted by permission of the Harvard Business Review. Copyright © 1982 by the President and Fellows of Harvard University; All rights reserved.

A World of Organization

We live in a period of rapid and powerful social and economic transformation, change not confined to the so-called capitalist or free-enterprise world but extending to the socialist countries as well. The transforming influence is organization. The growth of organization is for all to see—all, that is, who are disposed to see. There is, first, large and pervasive governmental organization. This can be a little larger or a bit smaller as liberals or conservatives will it; but government remains, as practical observers must agree, very large.

Organization extends to very large corporations; in the United States a couple of thousand companies now supply approximately two-thirds of all private products. A similar concentration is evident in the other industrial countries. Not everyone likes big corporations (multinationals are viewed with a particular suspicion), but they are here to stay. For complex tasks and for modern international trade, where the producer must follow the product with salesmanship and service to the ultimate customer, no alternative exists.

Where there are large corporations, there are, with the rarest exceptions, strong trade unions which, even if disliked, are also here to stay. Equally permanent fixtures on the scene are politically well-wired farm organizations, which in all industrial countries have succeeded in having a floor placed under most farm prices. And finally, if less fearsome than in the past, there is OPEC.

All of this organization has a common purpose, one that even those conditioned to the mystique of the market cannot wholly deny—that is, to take power away from the market and lodge it in greater or lesser measure in the hands of those who produce the product or service. This is a necessary, indeed an indispensable, feature of economic development. Modern corporate planning requires that, to the extent possible, future prices be subject to intelligent influence, if not control. The price prospect cannot be purely random. And the same is true of costs. And of the consumer response—that is what modern advertising and merchandising are all about.

Modern large-scale production, with its enormous investment and its long time horizons, would be impossible were prices, costs, and sales volume left to the uninhibited and wholly unpredictable movements of the classical free market. Equally, it is the purpose of farmers, oil producers, and workers to escape from the hazards and, on occasion, the cruelties of the market. The free and untrammeled market is greatly praised in the rhetoric; obeisance is rendered to it all over the industrial world; it is by no means dead. But the modern reality is a massive escape from its unpredictability.

It is the unsolved problems of a world of great organizations that lie back of our present travail. It does not help that market theology causes some governments, including our own in the United States, to approach this world as though it did not exist.

The unsolved problems are both external and internal. The internal ones are those of management, bureaucracy, and the bureaucratic dynamic, and they afflict both public and private organizations. The external ones, my present concern, are in the interorganization dynamic, as it may be called, for it is the tendency of organizations to interact to drive up costs and prices. Trade union claims and settlements shove up prices; rising prices bring further trade union claims; farm prices are adjusted upward and the higher living costs act on wages; energy prices contribute to the upward spiral.

All this is a visible and accepted fact of life in every industrial country. It is the modern form of inflation, the form inevitable in a world of organization. Prices can still rise as the result of the pressure of demand; but they also now rise, and more persistently, as the result of the interacting dynamic of prices and costs that have passed from the authority of the market to that of organization. And there is yet a further problem arising from the way in which, most notably in the United Kingdom and the United States, this new form of inflation is being countered.

Three Kinds of Policy

There are three ways and only three ways by which inflation, however induced, can be resisted. The first is by budget restraint—that is, a curtailment of spending and respending from publicly borrowed funds. This is fiscal policy. The second is by the curtailment of spending and respending from bank-borrowed funds. This is monetary policy. The third is by some form of direct intervention to restrain the pressure of trade union wages on prices and of prices on wages, thus stopping the interacting upward spiral. The problem of economic policy in an age of organization lies in the choice among these three instruments and their combination in what has come to be called macroeconomic policy.

In the English-speaking countries, direct intervention on wages and prices—an incomes or incomes and prices policy— is sharply in conflict with accepted market theology. If you are to have free markets, obviously you cannot intervene to restrain incomes and prices and thus counter the wage-price spiral. It will be said that the organizations to which I have just adverted have already undermined and made obsolescent the free-market assumption. That is true, but it is the nature of the devout free-market faith that it can transcend such circumstance.

Fiscal restraint—the need for limitations on public borrowing and spending to counter inflation—is accepted in principle in the modern world, but the powerful organizational dynamic of the modern state and the pressure of organizational power on modern government have made fiscal policy awkward, inelastic, and unpalatable. The services of the state are an important part of the standard of living; their reduction is strongly resisted.

Many of these services work to take the rough edges off capitalism—to supply income, medical care, housing, and transportation to the needy—and are thus in the interests of social tranquility. Some, not excluding military expenditure, are powerfully defended by strong public and private organizations.

The Reagan administration is providing a classic example of the perverse tendency of fiscal policy. It came to power with a strong avowal of its commitment to fiscal austerity and restraint. Yielding to the organized pressures for tax reduction, for larger farm expenditures, and for greatly increased military spending, it now faces deficits and resulting public borrowing on an unprecedented scale. Some of its economists, in one of the more spectacular manifestations of flexibility in the official mind, have even discovered that the public deficit, however large, does not cause inflation and is a quite normal exemplification of conservative finance.

With direct restraint on the wage-price spiral excluded by market theology and fiscal policy excluded by organizational and political pressures, there remains only monetary policy. This, in the United States as also in Britain, is the policy of choice; more important, it is the residual legatee in the action against inflation. There is no need, some professional vested interest of my fellow economists apart, to make economics more complicated than it is. We can understand nearly everything about the economic prospect for the United States, and by extension for much of the industrial world, by this commitment to monetary policy.

Triumph Over Self-Interest

Monetary policy does work against inflation, is working in the United States now. But it is a policy that works without severe pain only in the preorganization economy. It is the belief of all rigorous monetarists that such an economy—the classical free market economy—does, in fact, still exist. It doesn't; the belief that it does derives not from observation but from faith. When monetary policy is brought to bear in a world of strong organizations, as now in the United States and Britain, it has consequences far different from what would be expected in a classical market economy. And those different circumstances are the reality of our time.

Monetary policy, to repeat, works against inflation as it restricts spending and respending from banks and other lending institutions—from the spending and respending of the money and money equivalents so created. In a world of strong organizations, the first effect of this constraint, we now know, is not on prices but on output and employment. Before wage and price increases are curtailed, the output/employment effect must be severe. Only substantial idle plant capacity and unemployment can arrest the upward thrust of wages and prices.

This is not a matter of theory; it is the clear recent experience of Britain and the clear and yet more recent experience of the United States. In other words, inflation yields to monetary policy in the modern industrial world only as such policy produces a relatively severe recession. No business exercise in faith or optimism should be allowed to negate this fact. So long as any government—and of present relevance, that of the United States—relies exclusively on monetary policy to control inflation, it will succeed against such inflation only as it induces a recession.

Nor is this all. The impact of the recession will not be evenly distributed. The curtailment of bank and other lending by which monetary restraint is imposed is brought about by high interest rates—interest rates high enough to discourage borrowing . These high rates are not neutral; those who do business on borrowed money and those who sell extensively on credit are singled out for particular punishment.

Housing and the whole construction industry, the automobile industry, the farm equipment industry, and small business generally are all suffering severely from monetarist constraint in the United States, precisely as one would expect. The same is true in Britain. American business executives in these industries still, one judges, support Mr. Reagan's economic policy; it is a remarkable triumph of political loyalty over enlightened self-interest.

Equally evident is the international effect of this reliance on monetary policy. The high interest rates required by the policy in the United States draw deposit funds from other countries; in doing so, they give other countries the choice between a protective resort to equally high rates or some form of exchange control. So far the American monetarist policy has resulted in defensive rates in the rest of the industrial world. It could lead to an individual or collective resort to exchange controls and a breakup of the international financial system.

The Supply-Side Fantasy

There is a further effect that darkens the picture: Mr. Reagan took office with a powerful commitment to the monetarists. But he also brought to Washington the economic convocation called the supply-side economists. These men believed, or in any case learned, that they could win applause by avowing that if taxes were drastically reduced on individuals and corporations, production would expand, public revenues would rise, and the public sector would be as well financed as before. Taxes, in their view, were a major constraining influence on economic effort and investment. The result of the supply-side fantasy was the large recent and prospective reductions in personal and corporate income taxes.

This description of the supply-side vision as fantasy is now widely accepted. It is visibly as well as logically impossible to combine an expansion of the economy, encouraged by tax reduction, with a contraction occasioned by the rigorous application of monetary policy. But also there is no evidence that past taxation was a greatly constraining influence on either business effort and initiative or investment. Because something is attractive in the rhetoric does not mean that it is effective in the statistics. (Indeed, the most influential economic officer in the Reagan administration, David Stockman, director of the Office of Management and Budget, has described the supply-side vision as a cover for the reduction of taxes in the upper-income brackets.)

The supply-side aberration, in combination with a sharp increase in military spending, has now placed in prospect very large budget deficits—public borrowing on an unprecedented peacetime scale. This means that, for restraining inflation, there will be less rather than more reliance on fiscal policy, more rather than less reliance on monetary policy. There will be more public borrowing with a further upward thrust in interest rates. Or if the monetary policy is insufficiently severe, which is a distinct possibility, more inflation will result.

This is not a happy prospect, but none other can be seriously anticipated. I do not think that anyone who accepts the plain logic of economics in our time, including the powerful fact of a highly organized world, can—whatever his or her political views or preferences—reach a greatly different conclusion.

Nor is my view at odds with the assessment being made by the financial markets and by Wall Street. There can be few communities more eager than the American financial world to see the economic policies of the Reagan administration succeed. But looking at the budget prospect, the rejection of an incomes and prices policy, and the continuing increased reliance on monetary policy, the securities markets have reached the same conclusions as here offered.

Incomes and Prices Policy

What is the hope for improvement and change? The signals, if they come, will be two. The first will be when the United States moves to a greater emphasis on fiscal policy and a lesser emphasis on monetary policy, something I would urge on the other industrial nations as well. Fiscal policy—that is, a tighter budget as an instrument for controlling demand and that part of inflation resulting from the pull of demand—is in every way (except in political ease) superior to monetary policy. It attacks consumption expenditure rather than investment expenditure and thus has a less damaging effect on productivity; it does not single out interest-sensitive industries for punishment; in its effect on the economy, it is more predictable; it does not, as does monetary policy, encounter the great modern difficulty of all central banks, which is in defining what money is and in controlling with precision what cannot be so defined.

We shall begin to see a better prospect when the governments of all the industrial countries move toward narrower budget deficits (or their elimination), lower interest rates, and easier lending conditions. It will be an especially agreeable day when the United States moves decisively in this direction.

There is room for political preference in how the deficit is reduced. I would urge—have urged—canceling the personal income tax reductions (certainly the one in 1983), withdrawing the corporate income tax concessions enacted in 1981, and taking a stern look at military expenditures after 1981, while being very cautious about cuts affecting the cities and the poor. The question of military expenditures, it should be noted, goes beyond economics to the issue of arms control and survival itself.

The other signal for change will be the adoption by the industrial countries of deliberate and specific incomes and prices polices. Japan, Germany, Austria, Switzerland, and other European states have largely accepted the necessity for them. Wage settlements in these countries are accommodated to what can be afforded from current prices. Britain and the United States, deterred in part by a much stronger commitment to classical economic ideology, are the laggards.

An incomes and prices policy accommodates to the logic of an economy in which great business and labor organizations have the power to press wage and price claims and thus to bring about the interacting upward spiral of wages and prices. Monetary and fiscal policy arrest this spiral only as they arrest expansion and growth and produce instead a recession. This is not a matter of theory but of hard British and American experience.

Direct restraint on wages and prices in the highly organized sector of the economy takes the burden of inflation control off monetary and fiscal policy and allows the economy to operate at more nearly full employment, more nearly full capacity, and with the growth and expansion that then result. An incomes and prices policy is not a radical step into the unknown; as noted, it is implicit or explicit in the policies of the other industrial countries. In a real sense we have one now working through a recession in a rigorous and damaging way. An incomes policy is an inevitable accommodation to the highly organized economies of our time.

Much argument to the contrary, a strong incomes and prices policy served us well during World War II; there is no memory of inflation from those years. It served again in the Korean War, yet again in more informal fashion in the Kennedy years, and for Richard Nixon. By the 1972 election such policy, the handiwork of stalwart conservatives, had brought unemployment to less than 5 percent of the labor force and the annual inflation rate to less than 5 percent. In all these periods, inflation resumed when the controls were lifted; however, it is hardly a case against a policy that it does not work when you do not have it.

Any future incomes and prices policy would be confined to the highly organized sector of the economy where industrial and trade union concentration (with their pattern-setting effects) has made it necessary and where the same concentration—a few thousand corporations, a few hundred labor contracts—makes it administratively possible.

I do not suggest that this course is either pleasant or easy; economic policy is always an exercise in hard choices. I do suggest that, in the most conservative sense, it is far superior to price stability achieved through extensive unemployment and widely distributed business hardship and bankruptcy. The adoption of such a policy by the United States will be a major turning point in the world economic prospect; no one should expect such a turning point until then. All the alternatives control inflation only by depressing the economy and sacrificing growth.

Ideology vs. Circumstance

Thus the context—one that I urge, with all appropriate modesty, be a part of practical business thinking. No one will see this as an exercise in optimism, but there is one glimmer of light. The controlling influence in economic policy, as increasingly we see, is not ideology but hard circumstance. Not even the most committed ideologist can resist circumstances in an enduring way if the suffering is sufficiently great.

The day will come when the monetarist and associated classical-market fantasies will fade, and we will discover that it is better to adjust to the modern world—that of great corporations, strong trade unions, a large government apparatus, and the other manifestations of organization in our time. Then we will have industrial economies that work not as now but as they should and must. I would urge that business executives, for whatever influence they exercise, not be restrained by ideology from helping to bring that day nearer.

THE 1982 TAX BILL[6]

There is an old saying we've all heard a thousand times about the weather and how everyone talks about it but no one does anything about it. Well, many of you must be feeling that way about the present state of our economy. Certainly there's a lot of talk about it, but I want you to know we are doing something about it. And the reason I wanted to talk to you is because you can help us do something about it.

[6] Address by Ronald Reagan, president of the United States. *Vital Speeches of the Day.* 48:674–676. S. 1, '82. Reprinted by permission.

Believe me, if some of you are confused, I can understand why. For some time, ever since we started planning the 1983 budget for the fiscal year beginning this coming Oct. 1, there has been a steady drumbeat of "reports" on what we're supposed to be doing.

I know you've read and heard on the news a variety of statements attributed to various "authoritative Government sources—who prefer not to have their names used." Well, I think you know my name, and I think I'm an "authoritative source," since I'm right in the middle of what's going on here in Washington. So I'd like to set the record straight on a few of the things you might have heard lately.

I'm sure you've heard that "we're proposing the largest single tax increase in history." The truth is: We are proposing nothing of the kind. Then there is the one that "our economic recovery program has failed, so I've abandoned it and turned to increasing taxes instead of trying to reduce Federal spending." Well, don't you believe that one either.

Yes, there is a tax bill before the Congress tied to a program of further cuts in spending. It is not, however, "the greatest single tax increase in history." Possibly it could be called the greatest tax reform in history, but it absolutely does not represent any reversal of policy or philosophy on the part of this Administration (or this President).

Now you may have heard that some special interests oppose this bill. And that's right—some do. As a matter of fact, some in the Congress of my own party object to this bill—and strongly. I am told by many that this bill is not politically popular, and it may not be. Why, then, do I support it? I support it because it's right for America. I support it because it's fair. I support it because it will, when combined with our cuts in Government spending, reduce interest rates and put more Americans back to work again.

You will recall that when our Administration came into office a year ago last January, we announced a plan for economic recovery. Recovery from what? From a 1980 recession that saw inflation in double-digit figures for two years in a row. It was 12.4 percent when we arrived. Interests rates had gone into outer space. They were at the highest they'd been in a hundred years with a prime rate that hit 21½ percent. There were almost 8 million Americans out of work, and in several hard-hit industrial states there already were pockets of unemployment reaching figures of 15, 18, and even 20 percent. The cost of government was increasing at a rate of 17 percent a year.

Well, weeks and weeks of negotiations resulted in a Congressional Budget Resolution combining revenue increases and further spending reductions. Revenues would increase over a three-year period by about $99 billion, and outlays in the same period would be reduced by $280 billion. As you can see, that figures out to about a 3-to-1 ratio—$3 less in outlays for each $1 of increased revenue. This compromise adds up to total over three years of a $380 billion reduction in budget deficits. And remember, our original tax reduction remains in place, which means your taxes will still be cut $335 billion in these next three years.

Now, let me take that $99 billion tax program apart, and you decide whether it is the "biggest tax increase in history."

Of the entire $99 billion, $32 billion is collection of tax owed under the present laws and which is not being paid. To all of you who are paying your tax, simple fairness says we should collect from those who are freeloading.

Roughly $48 billion of the $99 billion represents closing off special-interest loopholes, which have resulted in unintended tax advantages for some, not all, taxpayers—some who are financially well able to pay their share. This is also a matter of simple fairness.

So more than 80 percent of the tax bill is not new tax at all but is better collection and correcting of flaws in the system.

This leaves $19 billion over three years of actual new taxes, which is far outweighted by the tax cuts which will benefit individuals. There is an excise tax on cigarettes and telephones. For people who smoke one pack a day this will mean an increase of only $2.40 a month. The telephone tax increase is only about 54 cents a month for the average household.

Right now, the tax reduction that we passed last year is saving the average family about $400 per year. Next year, even after this new tax bill is passed, the savings will almost double—$788. And here is what the totals look like: The new tax reform will raise, in three years, about $99 billion.

In the same three years, as I said a moment ago, our tax-cut program—even after this increase—will save you $335 billion.

Within the new bill there has, of course, been disagreement over some of the specific provisions. For example, there is considerable confusion over the proposal to have withholding of tax due on interest and dividends, just as it is withheld now on wages and salaries. Many senior citizens have been led to believe this is a new tax added on top of the present income tax. There is no truth whatsoever to that.

We have found that, while the overwhelming majority of Americans faithfully reports income from interest and dividends and pays taxes on it, some do not. It is one of the significant areas of noncompliance (and is costing the Government $9 billion a year).

In the case of those over age 65, withholding will only apply to those with incomes of $14,450 and up per individual and $24,-214 for couples filing a joint return. Low-income citizens below 65 will be exempt if their income is less than about $8,000 for an individual or $15,300 for those filing joint returns. And there will be an exemption for all interest payments of $150 or less. The only people whose taxes will be increased by this withholding are those who presently are evading their fair share of the tax burden. Once again, we are striving to see that all taxpayers are treated fairly.

This withholding will go into effect next July, not this January First, as was earlier reported.

There was little we could do about the budget already in place, but we could do something about the one that had been proposed for the fiscal year beginning in October of our first year.

I had campaigned on the belief that government costs should be reduced and that the percentage of the people's earnings taken by government in taxes should also be reduced. I also said that one area of government spending could not be reduced but must, instead, be increased. That was the spending necessary to restore our nation's defenses, which had been allowed to deteriorate to a dangerous degree in the preceding four years.

Interest rates continued high as the months went by and unemployment increased, particularly in the automobile industry and housing construction. Few could, or would afford the high interest rates for home mortgages or installment buying of an automobile. Meantime, we were putting our economic recovery program in place.

It wasn't easy. We didn't get all the cuts we wanted, and we got some tax measures we didn't want. But we were charting a complete turnaround in Government policy, and we did get the major part of what we proposed. The Congress mandated spending cuts of $130 billion over three years and adopted the biggest tax cut in history. This, too, was to be implemented over a three-year period. It began with a 5 percent cut in the personal income tax beginning Oct. 1, 1981, then a 10 percent cut this last July and another scheduled for July 1, 1983. These will be followed by indexing of the tax brackets so workers getting cost-of-living pay raises won't be moved up into higher brackets. You have to realize inflation itself is a tax. Government has profited by inflation—and indexing will put a stop to that.

There were tax cuts for business and industry to help provide capital for modernization of plant and equipment, changes in the estate tax, capital gains tax and the marriage penalty tax.

Some who supported us on the spending cuts were fearful of cutting taxes in view of the continuing budget deficits. We felt the tax cuts had to be a part of our plan in order to provide incentive for individuals and for business to increase productivity and thus create jobs for the unemployed.

It has only been 10 months since the first phase of our program went into effect. As I said earlier, there are those who say it has been tried and failed. Well, as Al Smith used to say, "Let's look at the record."

Start with interest rates—the basic cause of the recent recession. The prime rate was $21\frac{1}{2}$ percent. Last week it was $14\frac{1}{2}$ percent, and, as of today, three major banks have lowered it to 14 percent. Last week 90-day Treasury bills were paying less than 9 percent interest. One year ago they were $15\frac{1}{2}$ percent. That double-digit inflation (12.4 percent) has been cut in half for the last six months. Real earnings are at last increasing for the first time in quite a while. Personal savings, which trended downward throughout the last decade, are increasing. This means more money in the pool of investment capital. This will help to further reduce interest rates.

All of this in 10 months hardly looks like a program failed to me. Oh, yes! I failed to mention that in the quarter just ended there was an increase in economic growth—the first such increase in a long time.

Our biggest problem—the last one to be solved in every recession—is unemployment. I understand how tough it is for those who are waiting for the jobs that come with recovery. We can have no rest until our neighbors, our fellow citizens who want to work are able, once again, to find jobs. Again, let me say, the main obstacle to their doing so is continued high interest rates. Those rates should be lower now than they are, with the success we've had in reducing inflation. Part of the problem is psychological—a pessimism in the money markets that we won't stay the course and continue lowering the cost of government. The projected increase in budget deficits has added to that pessimism and fear.

And this brings us back to that so called "greatest tax increase in history" and the budget proposals now before the Congress.

When I submitted the 1983 budget to the Congress in February, it contained very significant spending cuts on top of those we obtained last year. This time, however, we could not get the support we had last year. Some who had not been happy about the tax cuts then were now insisting we must have additional tax revenues.

In fact, they wanted to cancel the reduction scheduled for next July and the indexing of tax brackets. Others proposed tax increases amounting to about $150 billion over a three-year period. On top of this, there was resistance to the spending reductions we asked for and even attempts to eliminate some of last year's cuts so as to actually increase spending.

For many months now we've been working to get a compromise budget that would further reduce spending and, thus, reduce the deficits. We also have stood firm on retaining the tax cuts already in place, because, as I said, they are essential to restoring the economy.

We did, however, agree to limited revenue increases so long as they didn't harm the incentive features of our economic recovery program. We ourselves, last year, had called attention to the possibility of better compliance with the tax laws—collecting taxes legitimately owned but which were not being paid.

Back during the campaign, on Sept. 9, 1980, to be exact, I said my goal was to reduce by 1985 the share of gross national product taken by government in taxes to 20.5 percent. If we had done nothing, it would have risen to about 24.8 percent. But even after passage of this bill, the Federal Government will only be taking 19.6 percent of the G.N.P. by 1985.

Make no mistake about it—this is a compromise. I had to swallow hard to agree to any revenue increase. But there are two sides to a compromise. Those who supported the increased revenues swallowed hard to accept $280 billion in outlay cuts. Others have accepted specific provisions with regard to taxes or spending cuts which they opposed.

There is a provision in the bill for extended unemployment payments in states particularly hard hit by unemployment. If this provision is not enacted, 2 million unemployed people will use up their benefits by the end of March.

I repeat: Much of this bill will make our tax system more fair for every American, especially those in lower-income brackets.

I am still dedicated to reducing the level of spending until it is within our income, and I still want to see the base of the economy broadened so that the individual's tax burden can be further reduced.

Over the years, growth in government and deficit spending have been built into our system. It would be nice if we could just cut that out of our system with a single sharp slice. That, however, can't be done without bringing great hardship down on many of our less fortunate neighbors who are not in a position to provide for themselves. None of us wants that.

Our effort to restore fiscal integrity and common sense to the Federal establishment is not limited to the budget cuts and tax policy. Vice President Bush heads up a task force that has been reviewing excessive regulations. Already enough unnecessary and duplicative regulations have been eliminated or revised to save an estimated $6 billion every year.

Our inspectors general have been mobilized into a task force aimed at ferreting out waste and fraud. They have conducted tens of thousands of audits, secured thousands of indictments resulting in many convictions. In the first six months of fiscal 1982 alone, they found $5.8 billion of savings and improved use of funds. Computer cross-checking has uncovered thousands of Government checks still going to people who have been dead for several years.

Task forces from the private sector are engaged in a study of the management structure of government. What they have learned already indicates a great potential for savings by simply bringing government procedures up to ordinary modern business standards.

Our Private Sector Initiatives Force, under William Verity, has uncovered hundreds of community and statewide projects performing services voluntarily that once were thought to be the province of government. Some of the most innovative have to do with job training and placement, particularly for young people.

What we need now is an end to the bickering here in the capital. We need the bipartisan comprehensive package of revenue increases and spending cuts now before the Congress to be passed.

We are not proposing a "quick fix"—an artificial stimulant to the economy, such as we have seen in the several recessions in recent years. The present recession is bottoming out without resorting to quick fixes. There will not be a sudden boom or upsurge. But slowly and surely we will have a sound and lasting recovery based on solid values and increased productivity and an end to deficit spending. It may not be easy, but it is the best way—the only way—to real and lasting prosperity for all our people. Think of it: We have only had one balanced budget in the last 20 years. Let's look forward to the day when we begin making payments to reduce the national debt instead of turning it all over to our children.

You helped us start this economic recovery program last year when you told your representatives you wanted it. You can help again—whether you are a Republican, a Democrat or an independent—by letting them know you want it continued, letting them know you understand that this legislation is a price worth paying for lower interest rates, economic recovery and more jobs.

The single most important question facing us tonight is: Do we reduce deficits and interest rates by raising revenue from those who are not now paying their fair share—or do we accept bigger budget deficits, higher interest rates and higher unemployment rates simply because we disagree on certain features of a legislative package which offers hope for millions of Americans at home, on the farm and in the workplace?

Do we tell these Americans to give up hope, that their Ship of State lies dead in the water because those entrusted with manning that ship can't agree on which sail to raise? We are within sight of the safe port of economic recovery. Do we make port or go aground on the shoals of selfishness, partisanship and just plain bullheadedness?

The measure the Congress is about to vote on, while not perfect in the eyes of any one of us, will bring us closer to the goal of a balanced budget, restored industrial power and employment for all who want to work. Together we can reach that goal.

BIBLIOGRAPHY

An asterisk (*) preceding a reference indicates that the article or part of it has been reprinted in this book.

BOOKS AND PAMPHLETS

Ackerman, Frank. Reaganomics: rhetoric vs. reality. South End Pr. '82.

Dye, Thomas R. Who's running America? The Reagan years. Prentice Hall. '83.

Evans, Rowland and Novak, Robert. The Reagan revolution: an inside look at the transformation of the U.S. government. Dutton. '81.

Heilbroner, Robert and Thurow, Lester. Economics explained. Prentice Hall. '82.

Valis, Wayne, ed. The future under President Reagan. Crown. '81.

Van Der Linden, Frank. The real Reagan. Morrow. 1981

Weintraub, Sidney and Goodstein, Marvin, eds. Reaganomics in the stagflation economy. U. of Penna. Pr. '83.

PERIODICALS

America. 146:114–115. F. 13, '82. Public need and the private sector.

Atlantic. 248:27+. D. '81. The education of David Stockman. William Greider.

*Atlantic. 250:8+. Jl. '82. Programs worth saving. Thomas F. Eagleton.

Business Week. p 26–27. Mr. 16, '81. Inflation sets policy once more.

Business Week. p 25. Jl. 13, '81. Why inflation's obituary is premature. S. H. Wildstrom.

Business Week. p 57–58. O. 26, '81. Heading for another budget showdown.

Business Week. p 46–47. N. 2, '81. Recession splits Reagan's team.

Business Week. p 134+. F. 15, '82. Reagan's blueprint for shrinking government.

Business Week. p 117. D. 6, '82. No recession for supply-side consultants.

Business Week. p 88. Ja. 31, '83. How strong a recovery?

*Business Week. p 25. Mr. 21, '83. Reaganomics II: More Keynes than Laffer. Seymour Zucker.

Business Week. p 106. Mr. 21, '83. Why the recovery may skip the farm belt.

*Commentary. 74:53–57. Jl. '82. What economists know. Melville J. Ulmer.

Commonweal. 108:452–453. Ag. 28, '81. Politics of taxes.

The Congressional Digest. 60:163+. Je./Jl. '81. President Reagan's tax-reduction proposal.

The Congressional Digest. 60:170+. Je./Jl. '81. Pros & cons. Should congress adopt the proposed three-year Reagan approach to federal tax reduction.

Forbes. 127:182–183. Mr. 16, '81. Year the bubble bursts. A. Bladen.

Forbes. 127:49. My. 11, '81. Reagan will get his tax cuts.

Forbes. 127:21. Je. 22, '81. What the near-term future holds? M. S. Forbes.

Fortune. 104:169–170. Ag. 10, '81. How the budget cutters cracked the whip.

Fortune. 105:42+. Ja. 11, '82. Eight questions for conservatives. Herbert Stein.

Fortune. 105:66–72. Je. 14, '82. How to bring interest rates down. A. F. Ehrbar.

Fortune. 105:77+. Je. 14, '82. Americans' hate affair with deficits. Everett Carll Ladd.

Fortune. 106:50–53. N. 15, '82. Stymied by the deficit. A. F. Ehrbar.

*Fortune. 107:77+. Ja. 24, '83. Has Reagan hurt the poor? Gurney Breckenfeld.

*Fortune. 107:67+. F. 21, '83. Reagan steps back from Reaganomics. A. F. Ehrbar.

Fortune. 107:133+. My. 16, '83. Chairman Feldstein lands running. Peter W. Bernstein.

Harper's. 264:8–10. Mr. '82. Waiting for Lenny. Stinginess masquerading as charity. Michael Kinsley.

*Harvard Business Review. p 6–12. Jl./Ag. '82. The way up from Reagan Economics. John Kenneth Galbraith.

*Harvard Business Review. p 60–71. Jl./Ag. '82. The desperate plight of the underclass. George C. Lodge and William R. Glass.

Macleans. 94:32. Mr. 30, '81. Hint of discord in the house. M. Posner.

Macleans. 94:28–29. Je. 15, '81. Overcome by the aroma of power. M. Posner.

Macleans. 94:43–44. D. 7, '81. Reagan's new trick. M. Posner.

The Nation. 233:102. Ag. 8–15, '81. Liberal dupes.

The Nation. 234:586–588. My. 15, '82. Where the health dollar really goes. J. Ehrenreich.

The Nation. 235:65+. Jl. 24–31, '82. Deregulatory agencies: Reaganism is harmful to your health. Michael Pertschuk.

The Nation. 236:559+. My. 7, '83. Carla: It's very hard to say I'm poor. Maxine Kumin.

*The Nation. 236:630–632. My. 21, '83. Big oil's stake in deregulation. Fred J. Cook.

National Review. 33:467–468. My. 1, '81. Reagan's other wound: the budget.

National Review. 33:605+. My. 29, '81. Kemp-Roth meets the O'Neill gang. D. Lambro.

National Review. 33:759+. Jl. 10, '81. Reagan coalition.

*National Review. 34:1074–1077. S. 3, '82. Reaganomics without Reagan. Joseph Sobran.

The New Republic. 185:7–8. Jl. 4–11, '81. Let them eat jellybeans.

The New Republic. 185:14–16. Jl. 25, '81. The shame of the Democrats. M. Kinsley.

The New Republic. 185:5–6. Ag. 15, '81. New gilded age.

The New Republic. 185:8+. S. 16, '81. Holiday hangover. M. Kondrake.

The New Republic. 185:5–7. O. 14, '81. Out on a limb.

*The New Republic. 187:11+. O. 18, '82. Urban enterprise fraud. James Traub.

The New Republic. 188:13+. Year end issue. '82. Unreal estate. Edward Abrahams.

The New Republic. 188:10–12. F. 14, '83. By deficits possessed. Jeff Faux.

*The New Republic. 188:14–17. Mr. 21, '83. The gang that can't deregulate. Mark Green.

The New Republic. 188:19–23. Ap. 18, '83. The laissez-faire elixir. Paul Starr.

The New York Times Magazine. p 12+. Ag. 9, '81. Taking charge of Congress. H. Smith.

New York Times Magazine. p 26+. O. 24, '82. Reagonomics and the president's men. Steven R. Weisman.

Newsweek. 97:43. Ap. 6, '81. Is the big tax cut dead? M. Beck.

Newsweek. 97:57–58. My. 4, '81. When good news is bad. W. D. Marbach and E. Newhall.

Newsweek. 98:20+. Jl. 27, '81. Hanging tough on taxes. P. Goldman.

Newsweek. 98:34–35. N. 16, '81. Goodbye balanced budget. T. Morganthau.

Newsweek. 98:36+. N. 30, '81. Playing budget 'chicken.' T. Morganthau.

Newsweek. 98:28+. D. 28, '81. Hell of a crunch in '82. G. Borger.

Newsweek. p 17–19. Ap. 19, '82. Reagan's polarized America.

*Reader's Digest. 123:59–64. Jl. '83. What really happened at EPA. James Nathan Miller.

Society. 19:33–38. Jl./Ag. '82. Reaganomics, reindustrialization and regionalism. Bernard L. Weinstein and John Rees.

Society. 19:39–43. Jl./Ag. '82. Assault on federal spending. Bruce Bartlett.

Society. 19:44–47. Jl./Ag. '82. Industry-growth sweepstakes. Bradley R. Schiller.

Society. 19:66–70. Jl./Ag. '82. New federalism and old facilities. Pat Choate.

*Society. 19:75–78. Jl./Ag. '82. Budgeting states' rights. Sar A. Levitan.

Society. 20:40–44. Ja./F. '83. Ronald Reagan: new deal conservative. Samuel H. Beer.

*Society. 20:45–48. Ja./F. '83. Retrenchment comes to Washington. Richard P. Nathan.

Time. 119:22. Ja. 11, '82. Looking back on a budget coup.

Time. 117:90+. F. 23, '81. Will Reagan's plan work? C. P. Alexander.

Time. 117:16+. Mr. 30, '81. Going Reagan billions better. G. J. Church.

Time. 117:16+. Je. 1, '81. Less than perfect. W. Isaacson.

Time. 117:46–48. Je. 1, '81. Outlook brightens.

Time. 117:10–12. Je. 15, '81. He'll do it his way. G. J. Church.

Time. 118:6–7. Jl. 6, '81. He got what he wanted. G. J. Church.

Time. 118:11. O. 5, '81. Stockman charge. D. Beckwith.

*Time. 119:19–20. F. 8, '82. New federalism or feudalism?

Time. 120:44+. S. 6, '82. Hope and worry for Reaganomics. George J. Church.

U.S. News & World Report. 90:18–19. F. 23, '81. Turn for the better?

U.S. News & World Report. 90:17. My. 18, '81. How Reagan wooed Congress.

U.S. News & World Report. 90:45. Je. 29, '81. Why U.S. is gaining economic heft. A. Zanker.

U.S. News & World Report. 91:25. Jl. 13, '81. Where inflation is leading us.

U.S. News & World Report. 91:27–29. O. 12, '81. How Reagan rates with Congress. C. R. Sheldon.

U.S. News & World Report. 91:58. O. 12, '81. Outlook for the year ahead.

*U.S. News & World Report. 92:26–27. Ap. 5, '82. A war Reagan's winning: taming the bureaucracy. David L. Barnett.

U.S. News & World Report. 92:39. Ap. 5, '82. Why supply side economics hasn't worked.

U.S. News & World Report. 94:18–21. Ja. 31, '83. Nine who hold key to Reagan's programs.

U.S. News & World Report. 94:66–71. Ja. 31, '83. How to get the country moving again.

Vital Speeches of the Day. 47:369–374. Ap. 1, '81. Preventing an economic calamity. E. Cornish.

*Vital Speeches of the Day. 48:523–525. Je. 15, '82. The challenge of less government. Robert Cizik.

*Vital Speeaches of the Day. 48:674–676. S. 1, '82. The 1982 tax bill. Ronald Reagan.

*Vital Speeches of the Day. 49:25–28. O. 15, '82. Can Reaganomics be salvaged? John O. Wilson.

Vital Speeches of the Day. 49:309–312. Mr. 1, '83. The American economy. William M. Agee.